CW00459635

Architecture of

Amerigo Marras, editor

Princeton Architectural Press, New York
StoreFront Books 3

Published by
Princeton Architectural Press
37 East 7th Street
New York, New York 10003
212.995.9620

For a free catalog of books published by Princeton Architectural Press,
call toll free 1.800.722.6657 or visit our web site at www.papress.com

Editing: Jan Cigliano
Design: Clare Jacobson & Brian Noyes
Special thanks to Eugenia Bell, Jane Garvie, Caroline Green, Therese Kelly,
Mark Lamster, Annie Nitschke, and Sara E. Stemen of Princeton Architectural Press.
—Kevin Lippert, publisher

ECO-TEC is the third publication of StoreFront Books, a
project of StoreFront for Art and Architecture, New York.
Amerigo Marras is editor and Tam Miller is associate editor.

Cataloging-in-Publication Data for this title is available from the Library of Congress

ISBN 1-56898-159-7 (pbk.)

Cover photograph: Mel Chin

Contents

Hybrids, Fusions, and Architecture of the In-Between

Amerigo Marras

This book is dedicated to the memory of two great Corsicans who contributed to the success of ECO-TEC, Pascal Le Grand and Felix Guattari.

The essays in this book are a small sample of the work produced by the series of international, interdisciplinary ECO-TEC conferences on the symbiosis between ecology and technology which have taken place since 1992, sponsored by StoreFront for Art & Architecture in New York. ECO-TEC became possible through initial organization by Jean Pierre Vernet in Corsica,[1] Roy Pelletier in Canada, and Kyong Park and Shirin Neshat in New York, and myself, as well as the ongoing collaboration with many participants from around the world.

The current discourse weaves ecology and technology in transformative flux. It not only searches for an ecologically sustainable architecture, it proposes as well a catalytic fusion between ecology and technology, intentionally generating some hybrid transgendering paradigms. Felix Guattari suggests that the basic question assailing us today is "how to produce, tap, enrich, and permanently reinvent (our subjectivity) in order to make it compatible with the Universe of changing values."[2] In this sense, *ecology* embraces the complexity of our social ecology, the ecology of the artificial environment that we produce in our being and becoming. It encompasses all ecologies that are at once natural and manmade.

The paradigm of ECO-TEC can be imagined as the transformation in one direction of ecology (*oykos-logos*) into a technolo-

Formalhaut, Cow Project, Vogelsberg, 1985 (A. Beck).

gy (*tekné-logos*), and a transformation of intelligent tools and designs based on the physics of nature, which evolve on a reverse trajectory. The architecture of ECO-TEC includes all the possibilities of this in-between conjunction of two diverging/converging reference points.

When I first proposed ECO-TEC in 1991, architects had been reluctant to include environmental awareness in their design practices, with few exceptions, such as DOMUS Academy's Ezio Manzini, the German Baubiology group, SITE, and Ove Arup in New York, with Postmodern and Deconstructivist preoccupations taking their momentary hold in mainstream discourse. Today, much has changed, and architecture and art more frequently include ecological and technological awareness. Indeed, our current social expectations and environmental quandary make us search for ecological applications of new technologies to solve ever greater and more troublesome environmental questions. The critique of our habitat requires re-examination of all technologies and their effects upon the world.

On one end of the spectrum, dogmatic ecological stances or Luddite criticism have limited usefulness, especially in light of another kind of tyranny, under the banner of a "clean" environment, which forged a political straightjacket, mass control, and economic stratification of social classes. On the other end, the uncritical acceptance of any machinic application, camouflaged as indispensable and, more dangerously, as inevitable, is equally to be criticized. To put it in perspective, let us not forget that even so-called simpler technological methods, like agriculture, domestication of animals, controlling fire and so forth, have upset nature through their application. We are searching for a far more complex involvement of communities and specialists in a context of informational wealth, not necessarily a simple return to nature.

Without entering into the discourse of "the end of nature,"[3] the state of our living humanity should include taking more direct control of our actions, the effects of which have been allowed until now to continue unabated, often to the point of great destruction. The relevant question should center on the degree of articulable intelligence of technology and the collective availability of knowledge and political control of our communities needed to build effective/affective damage-controls of our habitats. "Effects"-turning-into-"affects" is a practice of effective technologies replaced by affective, responsive, and collectively accessible methods. The true issue involves harnessing the political willpower to involve an educated community in the determination of its future and its economy. In the age of "intelligent machines," of totalizing supersensitive space satellites, of eavesdropping on vast territories and scopes, the colonization of the planet is now complete. This exhaustion of territorial conquest creates new pressures and re-proposes the question of what constitutes a community and what is an environment/ecology. Our technological culture is one ecology, one of the many possible ecologies.

We are forced to re-examine the long-assumed autonomy of the philosophies of architecture and of art. Less than a generation ago, in the late 1980s, young and brave architects, calling themselves "machine architects," modeled their strategy after the early Futuro/Modernists; they sought to escape from the revolving door of ineffective and reactionary pseudo historicism[4] by re-engaging technology at the center of their strategy. As exciting as this discourse was at the time, it never once raised the issue of ecological damage brought by technological applications, or of the widespread "sick building" syndrome. Yet, I felt that the discontent of this generation was genuine and could plug into a wider, ecologically sensitive discourse. The organizers of ECO-TEC invited such experimental thinkers as Neil Denari, who is the most visible exponent of the early machine-architecture movement, and designers at LaVillette School of Architecture in Paris and Paul Virilio's *Avant Traveaux*, to participate in a collective search of well-placed questions about the future of design and the environment. Today, I take satisfaction from the increased level of awareness and the transformation in the work of that generation of architects and critics. In fact, such talented young architects as Neil Denari or Dennis Dollens, among many, have created an architecture of the in-between based on new, sophisticated architectural paradigms in which ecology and technology intentionally intermesh.

Retooling our praxis is sometimes a solitary process of absorbing and incorporating a previously ignored awareness of social and natural ecology. It can be additionally empowered by collaborative work, in which many disciplines interface, to adopt methods of the sciences of complexity, chaos theory, fuzzy thinking, meteorology, biology, and geology, and to articulate intelligent and sustainable designs. The latter is often missing, for instance, in some recent mainstream architectural practice, although impressive in its scale and expanse, which has been defined as "Eco-Tech."[5] Merging disciplines and expertises should help us grasp complex whole issues, for example, connecting micro-effects with macro-transformations, the global with the local context, the urban with the unbuilt territory, and so forth.

Another important methodological lesson is the relevance of shifting the position of "the center" with that of "the margins"; the two are interrelated and interdependent, and not simply separate levels of power. An example of this approach is represented here by Mel Chin's sniper-viral strategy, first presented at the 1993 ECO-TEC conference on "Artificial Ecology." Chin's unusual performance-cum-manifesto explores the possibility of infiltrating unexpected contexts with encoded messages to sensitize mainstream culture. Several years later, Chin developed this idea into a public art project for the popular media, "In the Name of the Place," a collaborative effort of information-loaded sculptures, paintings, and props that were installed on the sets of the popular television show *Melrose Place*.

Although there is similar quest and history in relation for "green architecture," "sustainable architecture," and "eco-tech," ECO-TEC suggests not the extreme positions of being either-or but the fluid process of the in-between. Each design solution is a synthesis of a greater amount of knowledge, as well as a reconsideration of the roles played by the architect and the community. Andrew Ross, a critic and author who has participated in several ECO-TEC forums, reflects that "at this point in the ecological crisis we should have learned a thing or two: a) that there are no laws in nature, only in human society; b) that scarcity is not a natural condition but a human creation." He adds, "technologies based on natural elements, or imitating natural processes, are no guarantee of health, sustainability, or even biodiversity.... Biomorphic houses designed according to botanical principles ... are just as fitting instruments of social apartheid as housing modeled on industrial factories."[6] The social environment, the artificial ecology of our urban reality, is our sustaining body where financial and political decisions are made about the remaining natural space.

ECO-TEC in its live incarnations has produced a whole series of debates, some placed in the nearly pristine but politically troubled land of Corsica, others focused on New York, the model of an overdeveloped city of cities, the naturalized layering of man-made geology. Topics ranged from the artificiality of the city to the economics and applications of telework in small or rural communities to the potentials and dangers of Nanotechnology. The 1992 conference was the first time that Nanotechnology was discussed in relation to architecture. Additional case studies, which we called "workshops," or applications from our conferences, have centered on specific issues, including:

—"The Water Reclamation Project," by Danish landscape architect Neils Lutzen, a water treatment and recycling technique that uses a series of terraces to purify and consolidate water supplies for reuse

—Mel Chin's "Heartfelt," a study of native Mediterranean plants and wool for the production of natural color dyes and felts

—"The Canari Study," a land rehabilitation plan for one of the world's largest asbestos mines and factories which has been abandoned for decades on Cap Corse.[7]

Several authors developed specific issues, which they had introduced at ECO-TEC conferences into published books and web sites.[8] All of these offer an opportunity to explore a spectrum of issues, and to investigate a number of delicate cases.

In the Corsican ECO-TEC experience, the architect has learned while imparting his/her experience, from the artist, the geographer, the social critic, the botanist, the geologist, the local producer, and inhabitants. It is a completely multi-disciplinary strategy. All of this may seem like a perfect picture. It was not. We occasionally encountered local opposition and ideological representations of diverging political groups. The 1998 killing of Claude Erignac, the Corsican Regional Prefect, by an arm of the Corsican Nationalist Insurgency (FLNC, Front National de Liberation Corse)[9] was a reminder that violence does not effectively resolve conflicts. Instead, we have seen the extent to which participatory social ecologies can and should create the mechanics for political transformation.

What is truly remarkable about the Corsican ECO-TEC experience, despite ideological differences among participants, is agreement on two of the key issues that must be addressed in addressing change: ecology and technological development.

Long is the list of ECO-TEC participants since 1992, and it will continue to expand with the establishment of an experimental research center in Corsica. A pilot academic program began in Spring–Summer 1998, in collaboration with APARTIR, a branch of La Villette School of Architecture, as a first step towards the establishment of the Research Center on Architecture, Art and the Environment based in Morsiglia, Corsica, at the site where the first ECO-TEC took place. A special thanks should be given to Jean Pierre Vernet, the director of ECO-TEC Corse, for his untiring enthusiasm, never failing to go beyond any obstacle for the love of Corsica. Thanks also to Roy Pelletier for prodding me to take the then unforseeable giant step in the direction of ECO-TEC; Shirin Neshat and Kyong Park, founders and directors of StoreFront for Art and Architecture in New York, for believing in my work and ideas; the Municipalities of Cap Corse and the Corsicans, far too many to name, for their beneficial critique and sincere welcome; the French and the U.S. governments, for their financial support of our ambitious international endeavors; and the team of experts from different parts of the world. Special thanks are given to Leslie Sherr, Gianfranco Mantegna, and Helen Nagge, who have worked on the initial editing of the texts in this book. Lastly, I would like to thank the publisher, Princeton Architectural Press, and Tam Miller, associate editor, who has embarked on the ECO-TEC voyage with untiring cheerfulness and great intelligence.

Corsican graffiti (Tam Miller).

1 See Jean Pierre Vernet, "Morsiglia, Pays et Monuments sans Pollution," *Combat Nature* no. 103 (Nov. 1993), Périgueux, France.
2 Felix Guattari, *Chaosmose*. (Paris: Edition Galilée, 1992).
3 Alexander Wilson, *The Culture of Nature* (Toronto: Blackwell, 1992).
4 Robert McCarter, ed., *Building Machines*, Pamphlet Architecture no. 12 (New York: Princeton Architectural Press, 1987).
5 Catherine Slessor, *Eco-Tech: Sustainable Architecture and High Technology* (New York: Thames and Hudson, 1997).
6 Andrew Ross, "Ecoculture," *Art Forum* XXXI no. 4 (Dec. 1992).
7 *Condé Nast Travel* magazine, Summer 1991. Ironically, the blue pebble beach at Canari which was produced as a by-product of asbestos mining, was defined as the most beautiful in the Mediterranean basin.
8 Manuel De Landa, *A Thousand Years of Non Linear History* (New York: Swerve Editions, 1997); Mark Dery, *Escape Velocity* (New York: Grove Press, 1996); Andrew Ross, *The Chicago Gangster Theory of Life, Nature's Debt to Society* (New York: Verso, 1994); sites@RT66.com; Richard Lowenberg http:/infozone.telluride.co.us/store/iz/Italy.html.
9 www Corsica-nazione@Corsica-nazione.com

Amerigo Marras is the founder of ECO-TEC. *As an architect and curator, he has produced multimedia cultural events since 1973.*

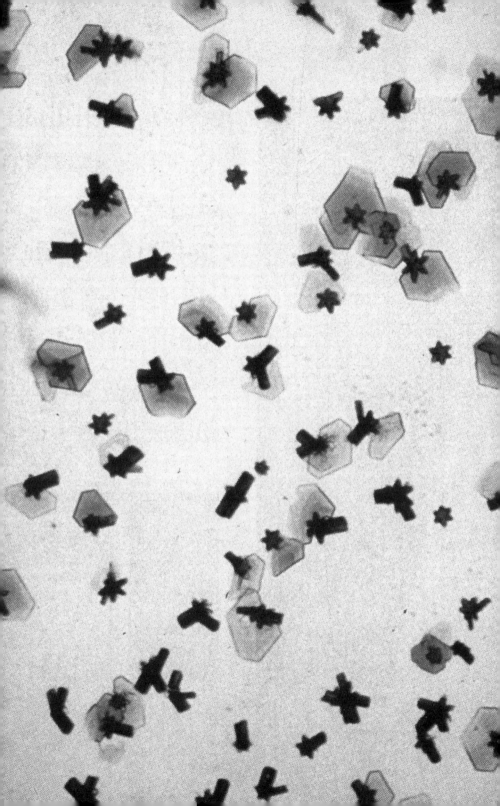

The Object of Ecosophy

Felix Guattari

Our geopolitical map is in the midst of rapid change, while techno-science, biology, computer technology, telematics, and the media destabilize our mental coordinates a little more each day. Poverty in the Third World, cancerous overpopulation, the monstrous growth and degradation of the urban fabric, the insidious destruction of the biosphere by pollutants, the incapacity of our present system to reshape social economy in keeping with the newest technologies: all these developments should have mobilized our minds, our sensibilities, and our will. But to the contrary, the acceleration of a history which may well carry us into the abyss is papered over by the banal and sensational imagery the media creates out of events.

The ecological crisis sends us back to a general crisis of society, politics, and existentialism. The task I would like to put before us in this essay is to commence a revolution in our philosophy, with the aim of no longer subscribing to an ideology of production that no longer bears any relation to human ends. How might we change our ways of thinking? How might we reinvent social practices that would give—or give back—to humanity the sense of its responsibility, not only for its own survival but also for the future of all life on this planet: the life of animal and plant species, to be sure, but also that of incorporeal

The first crystals of solid fullerenes (C_{60}/C_{70}) grown from a benzene solution. The larger platelets are about 25 micrometers across. Three crystalline forms-plates, rods, and stars can be seen. Pure C_{60} tends to form needles. Fullerenes are artificially created in the laboratory and promise advanced technological application (D. Huffman and W. Krätschmer).

species such as music, the arts, the cinema, ways of relating to time, love, and compassion, and the feeling of one's own fusion with the cosmos?

It is time for us to devise new means of collective organization and action relevant to a historical situation in which traditional ideologies and social and political practices have been subject to radical devaluation. While the new tools of information storage may well contribute to the renewal of invention and intervention, information technology alone will not produce the creative sparks to awaken new constructive perspectives. Starting from fragmentary projects, from sometimes precarious initiatives, from groping experiments, new collective agencies of utterance now begin to be sought. Other ways of seeing and making the world, other ways of being and producing new modalities of being, will open up and irrigate one another in a mutually enriching process. It is less a matter of attaining novel spheres of cognition than it is of creating mutant existential virtualities in a pathic mode.

This way of taking the subjective factors of history into account, and the ethical leap into freedom that results from the promotion of a genuine ecology of the virtual, do not in the least imply a turning-in on oneself (such as Transcendental Meditation) or a renunciation of political engagement. To the contrary, this way of thinking demands a refounding of the varieties of political practice.

Since the end of the eighteenth century, the impact of science and technology on developed societies has carried with it an ideological, social, and political polarization between progressive tendencies—which often perceived the State in Jacobinist terms—and conservative tendencies advocating a return to the values of the past. In the name of Enlightenment, of liberty, of progress, and finally of the emancipation of the working class, the basic references of social life have tended to align along expressed left-right axes.

Today, social democracies have embraced the primacy of the market economy, if not laissez-faire capitalism. The general collapse of the international communist movement has left a void in one of the extremes of the left-right polarity. Under these conditions, does it seem that the polarity of left and right is bound

THE OBJECT OF ECOSOPHY

to vanish, as the slogan of certain environmentalists, "neither left nor right," urges us to believe? Would that not be a way of inducing social life itself to evaporate like an illusion, as some proponents of Postmodernism have maintained? It appears that a reconstituted polarization will emerge in more complex patterns, more in the federal style than the Jacobin, a style which encourages dissent. On the other side, in response, remodelings of conservatism, centrism, and even neofascism will take form. The traditional party organizations are too closely enmeshed in the various mechanisms of the State to disappear abruptly from the systems of parliamentary democracy, despite the obvious loss of credibility which may be seen in the growing apathy of the electorate. Electoral contests as mediatic mass maneuvers and "politics of, by, and for the politicians" are on the way out, to be replaced by a new kind of social and political practice better suited to the most specific local questions and to the planetary problems of our age.

A more widespread ecological awareness, reaching much farther than the electoral influence of the "green" parties, should logically have led us to question the ideology of "production-for-the-sake-of-production," for example, production entirely centered on profit in the capitalist price-system and crippling consumerism. The aim would no longer be to take control of state power in place of the currently ruling bourgeoisies and bureaucracies, but to determine precisely what should be put in their place. On this point, two complementary themes seem to merit pride of place in future debates on the refashioning of a progressive cartography: the first is the redefinition of State functions, which are in reality multiple, heterogeneous, and often mutually contradictory; and the second is the deconstruction of the concept of the market, and the recentering of economic activity on the production of subjectivity.

In recent years, the neo-laissez-faire myth of the world market has built up an extraordinary suggestive power. To hear its proponents talk, merely to subordinate any economic grouping at all to its rule would be enough to make all its problems magically disappear.

In fact, there is no such thing as a hegemonic world market; there are only market sectors, each corresponding to a power structure. The finance market, the oil market, the housing market, the arms market, the drug market, and the not-for-profit sector, and so on, have neither the same structure nor the same ontological texture. They fit together through the balance of forces that have grown up among the power structures sustaining them. Today, a new structure of ecological power is emerging and, consecutively, a new ecological industry begins to carve out a niche among the other capitalistic markets. Heterogenetic systems of value—which counterbalance the homogenetic tendency of capitalism—need to consolidate their own structures of power, which will actively engage in new rapports of power rather than passively objecting to the misdeeds of the world market. Artistic arrangements, for example, ought to organize so as not to be the helpless servants of a finance market which in turn is symbiotically linked with the drug market. Education, as well, should not remain dependent solely on the State. It is time to develop alternative markets that would value a new quality of urban life, to a post-mass-media form of communication. To explode the absurdity of the hegemony of the capitalist system of values on the world market is, then, a way of giving consistency to Universes of value in social arrangements and existential Territories which go against the grain of the implosive evolution of the present moment.

So as to counter reductionist approaches to subjectivity, we have proposed an analysis of complexity that begins with a four-dimensional ecosophic object. Its dimensions are:

—material, energetic, and semiotic Fluxes;
—concrete and abstract Machinic Phyla;
—virtual Universes of value;
—finite existential Territories.

The ecosystematic approach to Fluxes represents an indispensable recognition of cybernetic interactions and retroactions relative to living organisms and social structures. But the question is also one of building a transversalist bridge among the totality of ontological strata which, each in its own way, are characterized by a specific figure of chaosmosis. These are the visible and actualized strata of material and energetic Fluxes, the strata of organic life, and also the incorporeal Universes of music, of mathematical ideal objects, of the Becoming of desire. This transversality is never a given, but needs always to be conquered through pragmatics of existence. Within each of these strata, of each of these Becomings and Universes, one finds a certain metabolism of the infinite, the menace of a transcendence, a politics of immanence. And each of these necessitates new schizoanalytic and ecosophic cartographies, wherever these elements exist and go unrecognized, wherever scientism, dogmatism, and technocracy forbid their emergence.

Chaosmosis does not presuppose an unvarying composition among the four ontological dimensions—Fluxes, Machinic Phyla, Universes, and Territories. Chaosmosis does not have any preestablished schemes; that is enough to distinguish it from the universal figures of catastrophe as found in the theory of René Thom. The cartographic representation of chaosmosis is part of a process of existential production based on elements of territorialized finitude, irreversible incarnation, processual singularity, and the engendering of Universes of virtuality which do not directly show up among the extrinsic coordinates of discourse. These elements come to exist through an ontological heterogenesis and declare their presence in the world of significations as a rupture of meaning and an existential reiteration. The positionality of these refrains in the ordinary world comes about, for example, as a derived and a significant function of mythic, literary, fantasmatic, and theoretical narrativity.

To speak of machines rather than drives, of Fluxes rather than the libido, of existential Territories rather than agencies of the self and transference, of incorporeal Universes rather than unconscious complexes and sublimation, of chaosmic entities rather than signifiers; to nest, circle-wise, ontological dimensions instead of splitting the world into infrastructure and superstructure—all this may not just be a question of vocabulary! Conceptual tools open and close fields of possibility; they catalyze virtual Universes. Their pragmatic consequences are often unforeseeable, faraway, slow in coming. Who knows what of this will be taken up by others, for other purposes, and to what crossroads it may lead?

Being becomes the ultimate object of a heterogenesis under the aegis of a new esthetic paradigm in the act of cartography and ecosophical metamodelization, activity which should occur in a style more modest and more audacious than that to which our educational system has become accustomed. It is more modest because this activity must give up any claim of its own permanence, of its unshakable scientific foundation, and more audacious because it may take part in the extraordinary race between machinic mutations and their subjective capitalization. Engagement in innovative social, aesthetic, and analytic activities thus implies crossing the threshold of speculative imagination, emanating not only from specialized theoreticians but also from enunciative orderings that now face the chaosmic transversality proper to the complexity of ecosophical objects. And in order to lay open ethico-political options relative to the microscopic aspects of the psyche and of social man, as well as to the global fate of the biosphere and the mechanosphere, we must make room for a permanent questioning of the ontological bases of every field's existing modes of valorization.

This cartographic activity can take on flesh in many ways. Deformed prefigurations include psychoanalytic therapy sessions; institutional analytic meetings; network activities; and socio-professional or neighborhood collectives. These practices have verbal expression in common. Speech ought to be an expressive vehicle of the individual psyche, the couple, the family, the neighborhood, the school, one's relation to time, to space, to animal life, and to sounds and sculptural forms. But verbal expression is not the only level on which ecosophy (or schizoanalytics) approaches its object. Many expressive mediums can be brought into the analytic arrangement, including postures, facial features, spatial configurations, rhythms, semiotic productions (which occur in monetary exchange), and the machinic productions of the sign. Speech itself enters only insofar as it grounds an existential refrain. The chief aim of ecosophical cartography will be, then, the production of enunciative arrangements that capture a situation's points of singularity. In this perspective, politically or culturally inspired meetings will find themselves called on to become analytic and, inversely, psychoanalytic work will be invited to take root in many micropolitical registers. The rupture of meaning—dissensus—will then become a privileged raw material, just as the symptom was for Freudianism. Personal problems, for example, should have a chance to emerge on the public or private stage of ecosophical enunciation.

In this regard, it is remarkable how ineffective the different groups of the French ecological movement have been in establishing a grassroots organization. The movement's whole object has been to form an environmental and political discourse. If you ask these ecologists what they intend to do to help the bums in their neighborhood, they generally answer that their responsibilities lie elsewhere. If you ask them how they expect to break out of their small-group habits and their dogmatism, many admit the question is justified but none can suggest a solution. Yet, in truth, their challenge is to help reinvent a progressive polarity, to rebuild politics on other bases, to make crosswise connections among private and public, social, environmental, and mental concerns. To make any headway in this direction, new types of cooperation, analysis, and organization need to take shape, perhaps on a small scale at first, then on a bigger one. If the French ecological movement fails to harness itself to this task of recreating political front-line organizations (collective arrangements of subjectivation), then there is little doubt that it will lose the public's confidence. The technical and interest-group side of technology will become the property of the traditional political parties, the State, and eco-business. Instead, the ecological movement should make a new social and mental ecology its prime concern.

Yet intellectual and artistic creativity, like the new social practices, have yet to win a democratic affirmation that would preserve their specificity and singularity. Prominent intellectuals and artists, formerly the prophets of existentialism, appear to have no lesson to offer. As to morality, there also appears no pedagogy of values. The Universes of beauty, truth, and goodness are inseparable from territorialized practices of expression. Values gain an apparently universal sway only when they are vehicled by Territories of practice, experience, and intensive power that connect them. It is because values are not permanently fixed in a heaven of transcendent Ideas that they can explode or catch themselves on catastrophic chaosmic stases.

Artistic cartographies have always been an essential element of the framework of our society. But ever since guilds of specialists arose to put them forth, they have come to seem an extra, a spiritual bonus, a fragile superstructure, the death of which is frequently announced. And yet, from the caves of Lascaux to the flowering of the cathedrals and on to SoHo, they have never ceased being a vital part of the crystallization of individual and collective subjectivities.

With art's framework attached to Social Man, it nonetheless carries its own weight. Every work has a double aim: to fit into a social network that will adopt or reject it; and to celebrate, once again, the Universe of art as that very Universe that is about to collapse.

Art's function of breaking with the trivial forms and meanings of the social field give art its status, that of permanence accompanied by the eclipse. The artist, and more generally aesthetic perception, detach and deterritorialize a segment of the real so as to make it play the part of a partial enunciator. Art endows a subset of the perceived world with a function of meaning and otherness. The work's nearly animistic breaking into speech has the effect of reshaping the subjectivity of the artist and of the "consumer" of art. The thing is to rarefy an enunciation which would be only too likely to drown in a seriality of identifications that would infantilize and annihilate it. For those who are accustomed to it, the art work is an enterprise of unframing, of the breaking of meaning, of baroque proliferation or extreme denudation, which draws the subject toward his or her own recreation and reinvention. On the basis of the artwork, a new existential propping will oscillate between the two registers of reterritorialization and resingularization. The event of the encounter with artworks may irreversibly mark the course of an existence and generate fields of possible "far off balances" of everyday life.

Seen from this existential function, from breaking away from signification and denotation, the usual aesthetic categorizations become irrelevant. What do such terms as *free figuration, abstraction, conceptualism* signify? What is significant is whether a work effectively contributes to a mutant production of enunciation. The focal point of artistic activity is, as ever, a surplus-value of subjectivity or the discovery of a negentropy amid the banality of the environment. Subjectivity has its consistency only through its renewal of a minimal resingularization, be it individual or collective.

The survival of our societies depends on research, innovation, and creation. These dimensions demand techniques of rupture and suture that are aesthetic in their nature. Something breaks away and works for its own sake as well as for others, if you are able to "agglomerate" yourself to that process. This sort of questioning concerns every institution, for example that of the school. How might a classroom be made to come alive like an artwork? What are the possible routes to its singularization, the source of the "grasping of existence" on the part of the children in it?[1] And in the register of what I once called "molecular revolutions," the Third World's treasures deserve exploring."[2]

It is time to reexamine the mechanic productions of image, sign, and artificial intelligence as new material for subjectivity. In the Middle Ages, art and technology took refuge in monasteries. Today it may be the artists who represent the farthest retreat-position of primordial existential questions: how to prepare these new fields of possibility? how to arrange sounds and forms in such a way that the subjectivity located next to them continues to move, that is, to live?

Contemporary subjectivity is not destined to live indefinitely turned inwards on itself, infantilized by the mass media, ignorant of difference and otherness in the human domain as well as in the cosmos. But its modes of subjectivization will never break free of their homogenetic siege unless creative aims appear within their reach. Here it is a question of the aim of all human activities. Beyond material and political demands there emerges an aspiration for individual and collective reappropriation of subjectivity. Thus the ontological heterogenesis of values is well on the way to becoming the nub of political rivalries which fail to address local matters, immediate relations, the environment, the rebuilding of the social fabric and the existential import of art. At the end of a gradual recomposition of subjectivation-arrangements, the chaosmic explorations of ecosophy, articulating scientific, political, environmental, and mental ecologies with one another, should be in a position to displace the old ideologies that split up the social, the private and the civil, being anyway profoundly incompetent to join politics, ethics, and aesthetics in a transversal cut.

This thesis does not advocate an aestheticization of Social Man. After all, the rise of a new aesthetic paradigm is bound to overturn existing forms of art as well as forms of social life. Our planet's trials, such as the choking of the atmosphere, require changes in our mode of production, our way of living and our axes of value. The demographic explosion that, over the next few decades, is expected to multiply by three the population of Latin America and by five that of Africa[3] is not the fruit of some biological curse. Economic factors of power and subjective influence, and cultural, social, and mass-media factors are the key to the problem. The future of the Third World depends on its ability to reassess its own process of subjectivation in the context of a progressively desertified social fabric.

In the fogs and miasmas that plague our end-of-the-millennium, the question of subjectivity emerges again and again like a leitmotiv. Subjectivity is no natural given, any more than air or water. How can we produce it, capture it, enrich it, constantly reinvent it so that it will be compatible with Universes of mutant values? How might we work towards its liberation, its resingularization? Professionals in the disciplines of psychoanalysis, institutional analysis, filmmaking, literature, poetry, urbanism, and architecture are responsible for combining their creativity to scatter the specters of barbarism, mental implosion, and chaosmic spasm which hover on the horizon, and to transform them into unpredictable riches and pleasures, the promise of which is, for the time being, entirely tangible.

1 Along the theme of institutional Pedagogy, see, among other works, René Laffitte, *Une journée dans une classe coopérative: le desir retrouvé* (Paris: Syros, 1985).
2 On the network of solidarity surviving among the "defeated" by modernity in the third world: Serge Latouche, *La Planéte des naufragés. Essai sur l'aprés-développement* (Paris: La Découverte, 1991).
3 Jacques Vallin (of INED), *Transversales Science/Culture* vol. 29 no. 9 (June 1991); *La Population mondiale, la population française* (Paris: La Découverte, 1991).

Felix Guattari, philosopher, died in 1992. He is the author of Chaosmose, *and coauthor with Gilles Deleuze of major studies on contemporary culture, notably* A Thousand Plateaus. *This essay was translated by Haun Saussy, and originally published in* Chaosmose, Edition Galilée, 1992.

THE OBJECT OF ECOSOPHY

Earth view of New York City, 1991. The dense urban development of the metropoli-tan area covering New York City, Long Island, and New Jersey shows up as gray and white on this infrared photograph (NASA photo).

The Nonlinear Development of Cities

Manuel De Landa

Cities as eco-systems may be defined as islands in two different senses. This applies not only to islands like Manhattan but to any city, even if it is landlocked. Climatologically, urban centers are heat islands, in the sense that they are appreciably warmer than the surrounding countryside. Concrete, asphalt, and other materials that make up a city's infrastructure retain heat; in addition, there are many heat-emitting devices in urban areas, such as air conditioners, cars, and agglomerations of people.

But cities are islands too, in the sense that their food webs (by definition, the eco-system) are extremely simplified just like those of islands. Urban centers house humans, domesticated plants, and animals; earth plants and animal "weeds" (such as sewer rats), and birds; and a varied insect lumpen-proletariat, of which the cockroach is the best example in Manhattan.

Because there are very few niches filled, islands tend to be unstable eco-systems and are therefore open to invasion by other species. Urban food webs inherit this lack of resiliency. This runs counter to the romantic view of cities held by nineteenth-century social thinkers, in which cities were seen as organisms in functional harmony.

Today we know that neither nature nor cities are in harmony, that is, in a static state of equilibrium. Both natural and social structures emerge in a complex dynamic process, which

Map of New York; Lithograph by George Hayward for D.I. Valentine's Manual, *1860.*

may involve changes from one stable state to another, from a steady stable state to a cyclic stable state, to a more chaotic stable state. Cities are unstable eco-systems far from equilibrium.

Historically, cities have always been parasitic entities; they have drawn on the countryside for their flow of food and human resources. Very few cities in the last ten-thousand years have survived more than seventy generations from this food parasitism. The main reason has been intensive agriculture and the concomitant erosion of the soil. The ancient Phoenicians cultivated terraces, thus demonstrating that the process of socializing the soil has existed for a long time. Yet very few urban centers made use of such devices and many died from not implementing conservation practices. The societies that did survive beyond seventy generations—for instance Mesopotamia and Egypt—did so not because of "social constructions" but because their own geographical conditions allowed them to survive longer on that soil—for example, a flat terrain that did not suffer from erosion. Cities have never really fed themselves.

And until recently, cities never reproduced themselves either. Until the nineteenth century, the index of mortality in most cities was higher than in the surrounding countryside, and urban mortality rates were higher than birth rates. One important reason for this was the prevalence of epidemic diseases, some of which thrive on a critical density of population and are specifically urban diseases. Because of this historically high mortality level, cities have depended on continuous migration from the countryside.

Cities have always been parasitic creatures, in short, surviving thanks to the inflow of food and of human genes. In this context, political and jurisdictional power can be exercised through biology. For instance, when cities run out of soil, or food, they colonize new territories; they send genes from their own gene pool to a different place, sometimes mixing with the natives, sometimes simply exterminating them. But even these invasions have a non-human, biological component. The reason that several million Aztecs lost against about thirty Spanish invaders in the early 1500s was due to the cultural advantages of the invaders' fire-weapons and domesticated animals. The Aztecs did not have fire weapons and were completely shocked by horses, which they had never seen. The Aztecs also believed in a legend that called for a blond god to appear one day; the Spaniard Hernando Cortés was blond. More important to their success than these cultural factors, however, the Spaniards brought epidemic diseases with them, such as smallpox and measles. Ninety percent of the Indian population in America was exterminated by epidemic diseases. Smallpox spread to the Incas before Pizarro even saw them. Those who survived were so demoralized that mass conversions to Christianity were almost a logical outcome. They saw white people surviving these diseases, and they believed there was validity in the myth claiming white peoples' superiority. If cultural anthropologists view human culture as a completely separate realm from biology, they ignore genetic facts and become as culpable as socio-biologists for whom biology is everything. Each discipline, to be sure, has its own agenda and both may ignore the complex interplay of biological and cultural elements, particularly in the case of urban centers.

The distinct cultural differences between individual cities may be seen in the differences between a metropolis and a capital: New York and Washington, D.C., for example. One way to conceptualize this difference, which is acquiring some currency, is to distinguish two types of structures that can appear both in the natural and the artificial world: one type of structure is known as "hierarchies of command and control"; the other as "self-organizing systems." Hierarchies of command and control, a major form of state structures, are also the framework for human DNA. Self-organizing processes, as well, may have natural and cultural manifestations. A self-organizing structure typically emerges without central planning, as a consequence of a decentralized process. For example, ant and termite colonies as well as pre-capitalist markets are self-organizing. In addition, certain parts of the body are strictly under genetic control, such as digestive and respiratory systems.

It is not a matter of the opposition of one to the other; nature is filled with mixtures of these two types of structure. What does matter is to determine which structure predominates. If the command hierarchy predominates, then homogeneous structures tend to prevail and alien (heterogeneous) elements are weeded out; everything is arranged into a hierarchy. If self-organizing processes predominate, then a more heterogeneous mixture of elements, an articulation of diversity prevails. This approach can be applied to the study of cities.

One should ask, why did China not dominate over the West, in light of its land and population size? One thousand years ago, the West was a very primitive place, dominated economically by Islam. China, by contrast, had invented gun powder, the compass, paper money, and moveable type for the printing press between 900 and 1000 A.D. These became the four cultural weapons the West later used to conquer the rest of the world. The West would prevail, however, for a variety of reasons, one of which was germs. Another reason was the dynamics of Western cities.

Cities, as mixtures of self-organizing and command hierarchies, tend to represent some combination of market (self-organizing) and the state or the state bureaucracy (command hierarchy). Markets have existed since there has been civilization. India's and China's first-century markets, before the British, Portuguese, or Dutch arrived, were extremely complex entities, self-organized in the most concrete sense. No one entity determined the flow of goods and a global order emerged spontaneously out of the interaction of many different agents. Centralization of economic power came later in history. Bureaucracies did interact with markets, to guarantee security, extract taxes, and set standard weights, but did not control them.

In the West, another entity emerged: big business. Beginning in fourteenth-century Italy, which was the birthplace of what we call capitalism, big business coexisted alongside the market but did not obey its pricing laws of self-organized supply and demand. Big business operated on a large scale, as in wholesale commerce, or monopolized a particular flow of spices or prestige goods. It never participated in the dynamics of the market, except to manipulate these dynamics. This is not a matter of stages of development, as the Marxists would want us to believe, as if big business was only characteristic of twentieth-century mature or late capitalism. That is why *anti-market* is a more appropriate term for big business; capitalism suggests a global system that permeates society through and through. Even today, anti-markets represent only fifty percent of the economy; they have never invaded the whole of society. One of the main traits of anti-market institutions is their ability to secure and to earn financial capital. They forfeit areas of business in which profit levels are below a certain threshold, leaving these to supply-demand markets.

Economic history is represented by a mixture of big business and the state, which have a high component of hierarchical command, and of supply-demand markets and other decentralized systems, which have a high component of self-organizing processes. In the same way, cities can be distinguished by the mixture of components that predominate: state capitals and market-based metropolises. Or, to be more specific, the state or royal towns of Cairo, Peking, Paris and Madrid, and the commercial towns of London, Venice and Amsterdam. Commercial towns always exist in networks, which may lack a distinct center. State towns, by comparison, are centers that tend to require the submission of other towns and into which wealth flows. Commercial towns are typically maritime, connected to the self-organizing processes of the seas and oceans. State towns are often landlocked and protected, such as Peking and Madrid. Commercial towns tend to free the flows of goods and services from obstacles, not to do good to humanity, but to exploit the countryside. Commercial towns, as highly heterogeneous formations, articulate diverse elements; state towns tend towards homogeneity of ideas and values. However, since different elements operate on different scales we can also find command hierarchies in the most commercial towns.

In New York City, for example, commercial and metropolitan elements tend to predominate. It is among a long list of towns which rose to become centers of the world economy in their time: Venice, Antwerp, Genoa, Amsterdam, and London. All were in direct contact with the ocean, with self-organizing currents and winds. The self-organizing winds, like the trade winds that brought Columbus to America, are huge convection cells, coherent flows that arise at a certain critical threshold in temperature differences. The centers of the world economy have always been metropolitan towns, not capital towns. When historian Fernand Braudel compared these commercial centers to Chinese or Islamic towns, he asked:

> What stopped the rest of the towns in the world from enjoying the same relative freedom? Why was change a striking feature of the destiny of Western towns, even their physical

existence was transformed, when the other cities had no history by comparison and seem to have been shut in long periods of immobility? Why were Western towns like steam engines, while the others were like clockwork? In short, comparative history compels us to look for the reasons for these differences and attempt to establish a dynamic pattern of turbulent urban evolution in the West while the pattern of life in cities, in the rest of the world, runs in a long straight and unbroken line across time.

Historian William McNeill, a pioneer of the history of diseases, in his book *The Pursuit of Power*, agreed with Braudel:

> In China, the command element in the mix remains securely dominant. Market behavior and private pursuit of wealth could only function within the limits defined by the political authorities. For this reason the auto-catalytic character that European, commercial and industrial expansion exhibited, between the 11th and 19th century, never got started in China.[1]

The term *auto-catalytic* is almost synonymous with the word turbulent that Braudel uses. An explosion is a typical example of an auto-catalytic process that catalyses or accelerates itself. An explosion is driven by heat and itself produces heat, which may be fed back into its own process; as gun powder burns, more heat is produced so more gun powder is burnt. It is a self-reinforcing reaction. Not all cases of auto-catalysis are explosions, but all can exhibit explosive or turbulent behavior. The technical term for this is a *positive feed-back loop*, in which small deviations are amplified and give rise to heterogeneity, or differences.

On the other hand we have *negative feed-back loops*, illustrated by the principle behind the thermostat. A thermostat reads the current temperature and compares it to the desired level, and changes the heater in the appropriate direction to bring room temperature to that level. A negative feed-back loop, unlike a positive feed-back loop, which is explosive or turbulent, dampens or eliminates deviations from the desired levels, hence promoting homogeneity. These two forms of circular causality are also present in the diverse processes that make up a city, so that towns may be considered mixtures of positive and negative feed-back loops. Their characters emerge from the kind of loop that predominates in the mixture.

To move to a more concrete plane we may ask what kind of turbulence entered into the mixture of towns like Venice in the middle ages, Amsterdam in the eighteenth century, London in the nineteenth century, and New York in the twentieth century. One possible answer is offered by urbanist Jane Jacobs in *Cities and the Wealth of Nations* (1984). There she suggests that the process driving these towns far from equilibrium, leading Western towns into a turbulent, auto-catalytic state, is "volatile trade."[2] Volatile trade occurs when a city, typically a part of a trading network, begins to replace imports by its own manufactured products and sets a whole series of self-reinforcing, positive feed-back loops into motion. To replace imports a city must develop new skills and procedures using its own human resources and local creativity. History suggests that this process, to be successful, has typically involved many small manufacturing firms, rather than a few large businesses. Economies of scale are achieved through large collections of small enterprises interacting with one another. Jacobs's hypothesis is that a dynamic process of "import-substitution" enabled eleventh-century Venice and fifteenth-century London to mature from being exporters of raw materials and importers of manufactured products, to become increasingly self-sufficient.

When a city begins to replace what it imports with local production, it stimulates the creation of skills, knowledge, and processes. If this happens within a network with a large enough number of firms which are competing against each other yet at the same time dependent upon one another, this becomes a self-reinforcing loop in which every new round of import-substitution generates new skills and procedures and the pool of knowledge grows in that city.

Jacobs is very critical of the current policies of the World Bank which simply funds industrialization in the Third World, regardless of the dynamics involved. For example, giving developing nations money to build dams, and other infrastructural projects, such as roads, ends up benefiting only local (or international) anti-markets, such as large corporations. These investments do not generate self-catalytic loops in cities and therefore, the Third World countries get stuck with a huge debt they can never repay. Corporations internalize the new knowledge that is produced and given their autonomy and freedom of movement, they can relocate somewhere else, leaving behind ghost towns or at least impoverishing the region.

Import-substitution dynamics involves not single cities but teams of cities, since at first the locally manufactured products are not of high quality and so need to be traded with other backward cities. New York belonged, in the eighteenth century, to such a network of import-replacing cities, a network encompassing Philadelphia and Boston plus a host of smaller towns. Replacing imports from Europe and building their own local reservoirs of knowledge, argues Jacobs, is what transformed these cities from British supply zones into independent urban centers stimulating each other's growth.

Unfortunately New York City does not exhibit these powerful dynamics any more, which is not to say that in other areas such as culture, it may still be very vital and vigorous. After World War II the mixture of dynamical processes we call New York experienced an increase in hierarchical command elements and a sharp decrease in its self-organizing components as small firms were squeezed out by bigger businesses.

According to Jacobs, the decline of cities began even before the establishment of big business—the moment they were digested by and incorporated into nation states, which also increased the command element in the mix. Cities need their own currencies to know how to balance import-export. If the value of the city's currency is low with respect to other cities, then its exports will be cheap. If its over-valued, with respect to other currencies, then its exports are expensive in other cities. Local currencies allow the creation of a negative feedback loop that stabilizes a city's import-export dynamics.

When cities were swallowed by nation states, starting in the sixteenth century, they lost this source of information, and the negative feed-back it drives, because a national currency was established. The nation as a whole was able to get negative feedback about its exports and imports but the networks of cities were not able to get this information. This was only one factor, however, in the increase of command elements. There are others but to understand the role they played we need to get rid of the notion of the "capitalist system" and view societies as composed of a more complex, more heterogeneous ecology of institutions. For a long time, for instance, it was thought that mass production techniques, à la Henry Ford were a creation of capitalism. Yet, some historians now argue that the basic elements of mass production started in military arsenals and armories in eighteenth-century France, and became institutionalized at the beginning of the nineteenth century in American armories, that is, a hundred years before Henry Ford applied them to the civilian industry. The problem the military faced was the need for weapons (rifles) with interchangeable parts, so that they could supply a battlefront with spare parts. But when craftsmen manufactured each rifle individually, it was not possible to take one part of a rifle and put it in another. So a whole new set of procedures, routines and methods was established, as well as the disciplinary means to enforce them.

The military did not simply export certain products to the civilian industry (Napoleon promoted the canned food industry and this may have benefited the civilian world), it exported the whole grid of command and control needed to produce products. It was this that increased the command element in the economic mix of the West, and that brought us to the situation where we find ourselves now, a world dominated by giant and global antimarkets. Yet, unless we locate the exact sources of the command hierarchical component in our mixture, and not just idealize an enemy with concepts like "the capitalist system," we will not be able to dismantle these oppressive structures and invent new institutional designs to replace them. The first step in this reconceptualization is to see urban centers as housing a heterogeneous mixture of institutions, a complex institutional ecology whose historical dynamics we are only beginning to understand.

1 William H. McNeill, The Pursuit of Power: Technology, Armed Force and Society since A.D. 1900 (Chicago: University of Chicago Press, 1982).
2 Jane Jacobs, Cities and the Wealth of Nations: Principles of Economic Life (New York: Random House, 1984).

Manuel de Landa is a filmmaker and author of War in the Age of Intelligent Machines and A Thousand Years of Non Linear History.

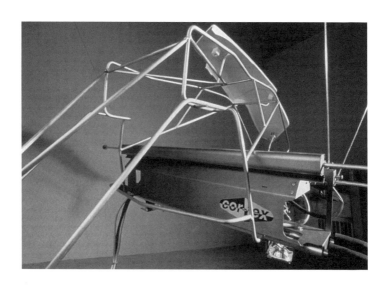

Smog Monster: Environmental Notes from the Pac-Rim

Neil Denari

1.0 On July 11, 1997, the South Coast Air Quality Management District (AQMD) adopted a regulation that constitutes one of the largest reductions in hydrocarbon emissions by requiring businesses to switch from petroleum-based to water-based degreasing solvents. More precisely, it is the single largest hydrocarbons emissions reduction measure adopted in eight years. The measure will reduce volatile organic compound (VOC) from solvent degreasing tanks by 76%, or 40.2 tons per day by 2010.

The AQMD attack on solvent use is logical as it is one of the largest sources of SMOG-forming VOC emissions in Southern California, equal to the combined emissions from every gas station, oil refinery, petroleum storage facility, and gasoline tank truck in the region.

2.0 SMOG is produced when the following four elements work together in a chemical fusion:

1. SUNLIGHT
2. The production of oxides of nitrogen (NOx)
3. The production of volatile organic compounds (VOC's)
4. A temperature greater than 18° C.

When the word SMOG was coined in London earlier in this century, it was formed clearly from a contraction of the words SMOKE and FOG. Yet, when one looks at the chemical make up of SMOG, the element of FOG (a cloudlike mass or layer of minute water droplets or ice crystals near the surface of the earth, appre-

Roizumi Birdhouse, 1993 (Benny Chan), above; Floating Illuminator, 1992 (Benny Chan), below.

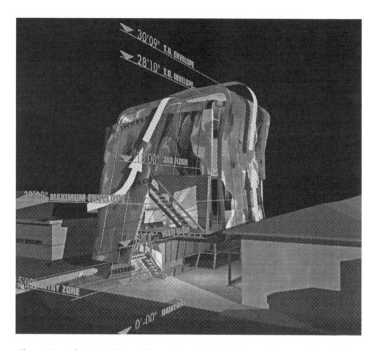

Flower Smooth, Vertical Smoothouse, Beverly Hills, CA, 1997. To expand an existing house, the author created a vertical addition between house and garage that maximizes the value of high-priced land and includes an office, sleeping/living area, bathrooms, kitchen, dining areas, and deck. The house is formed by a single curving sheet which describes the basic envelope of the house. The sheet bends into itself, creating invelopes, or internal surfaces which merge seamlessly with the exterior. A structural steel frame supports the sheet and is hidden within an outer layer of standing seam metal and an inner layer of gypsum plaster. Design assistants: Carsen Primdahl, John Hartmann, Rebecca Rudloph (Neil Denari).

ciably reducing visibility) is not part of the equation. As light and heat meet volatile chemicals, FOG is more likely to be invoked as the dominant (and only) operative in this pair of climatological phenomena. Hardly twins, SMOKE and FOG emerge from vastly different places, one the production of deliberate conditions orchestrated in the industrial world, the other a seemingly benign production of weather patterns. Seen as vague, evanescent vapors, they become much more reflexive of one another. Yet, why assign FOG (nature) an accomplice role in the horror of polluted skies? Is it because fog or marine layers collide with the industrial world in a way which, rather than diluting the chemi-

cal haze, actually turns it into something much more unhealthy?
3.0 Each year, in the Moreno Valley of central California, along Interstate 5, the FOG becomes so dense that at least one major auto pile-up occurs. Massive chain reactions of rear-end collisions are the result of momentary reductions of visibility where perception and control disappear at the hands of nature. Unable to locate the cars in near proximity, drivers are overcome with a kind of "natural blindness." A number of deaths are recorded each year in these dangerous conditions.
4.0 Researchers in Southern California in 1997 provided clear medical evidence that all people experience SMOG differently due to genetic make-up. Where some individuals become violently ill from the noxious air of a region, others have no physical reaction at all and do not suffer any bodily degradation from the chemical environment of FOG.
5.0 If ECOLOGY is the branch of biology dealing with the relations between organisms and their environments, then SMOG is not a product of technology. It is, in fact, a defining condition of ecology itself, one that sets out to extinguish all culpability in the crisis of the environment. Since the overwhelming beauty of the found landscape and the forces that shape it (all sublime and dangerous) intersect with the built environment in not always productive ways, the hazards of the environment may themselves be products of a collaboration of natural and technical conditions which require a new "politics of convergence" instead of the prevailing one of antagonism.
5.1 The paradigms of the MECHANICAL (technology) and the FLUID (nature) are projected as opposite modes of thought and the latter has not only been perceived but in fact welcomed as having supplanted the former as the prevailing structure. With this ushering in of a new, more supple paradigm, we are now involved in the further extrapolations and submissiveness to the temptations of what Armand and Michelle Mattelart call "the whole parade of metaphors."[1] If the fluid model is one which overcomes the causal and linear systems of thought that MECHANICAL progress seeks to destroy, then, as the authors reluctantly suggest, "the new paradigm of the fluid can only be interpreted with ambivalence–ambivalently and in an open manner, just as we perceive the formation of micro- and macro- uses of communications technologies."[2]

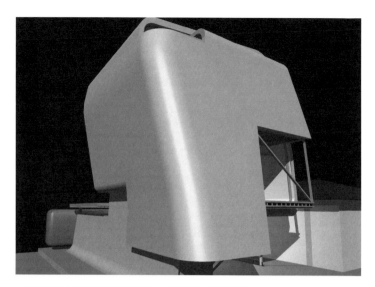

Prototype for high-rise building. Neil Denari, architect. Vertical Weekly Mansion, Tokyo, 1994-96. This project is STRAIGHTFORWARD ARCHITECTURE. The zoning envelope in Tokyo allows a vertical extrusion up to 30 meters. Above that, the building mass must slope back by 45 degrees. With this small site, there is no room to slope back above the site perimeter. Floor area ratios, budgets, and strictly enforced earthquake structures all seem to determine the conventional building in Tokyo. This high-rise prototype, instead, treats the interior apartment as an industrial design where aluminum tables and futons are concealed in the floor surface for temporary pop-up use. Each apartment contains video projection and flatscreen LCD wall panels. The structure is a reinforced concrete service core acting as the main column with steel framed floors and bracing for the units. Steel stairs are cantilevered from the rearside of the concrete core. Electron inverting glass and aluminum panels are the main external cladding materials. Section (above); Entrance (below). Assistants: Irene Lai, Gunther Schatz, John Hartmann (Neil Denari).

The Mattelart's go on to say that "with the paradigm of the fluid, something was fractured: the image of power located at a single point in society, visible and unambiguous–the image of a central power perfectly articulated with its periphery. The emerging image is one of complex networks of places, whose very entanglement makes decision-making complex." [3]

The schema of mechanical thought, and all of its various formal metaphors and deployments of force, have been undermined by the powerful yet highly ambiguous possibilities of the fluid. Nonetheless, the fallout of this challenge to the stable structures of the mechanical have produced a NEW RELATION among forces, not the eclipsing of a seemingly outmoded system of thought.

In his introduction to *The System of Objects*, Jean Baudrillard identifies the "technological plane" as an abstract surface above the "spoken" or accepted plane of meanings of objects.[4] He reminds us how unconscious we are of the technological reality of objects. In use, technology is rather transparent, but as spent icons, it is the site of guilt or political hindsight . . . it no longer seems abstract to us. It was Michelangelo Antonioni (*L' Eclisse* or *Il Deserto Rosso*) and J.G. Ballard (*High Rise* or *Rushing to Paradise*) who understood that technology is a part of culture, that it defines its intentions very well, whether for pleasure, destruction, or any other function. Their work is not heavily judgmental on the surface. However, as they expose the technological landscapes around us, it is impossible not to read into the particular, if subtle, prejudices at work. This is where ambivalence becomes such a powerful emotion. The corrupted optimism of this century is visceral, of space-age ideals which have mutated into provisional and momentary flashes of beauty. What is interesting is that they have portrayed the disaster as more a product of our own paranoia than of machines gone wrong.

1 Armand and Michele Mattelart, *Rethinking Media Theory* (St. Paul: University of Minnesota Press, 1992), 48.
2 Ibid., 53.
3 Ibid., 57.
4 Jean Baudrillard, *The System of Objects* (London: Verso, 1996), 4.

Neil Denari, architect, is Director of Southern California Institute of Architecture.

Recycling Recycling
Mark Wigley

What is it to talk about ecology and architecture again? Why recycle ideas about recycling? Hasn't it all been said before? Did we miss something? Or forget it too quickly? The discourse of the not-so-distant past is a precious but unstable resource. Redistributing it requires utmost care.

Take two books on ecology from the end of the 1960s: *The Future of the Future* of 1969 and *The Ecological Context* of 1970. Written by the sociologist John McHale, these influential manifestos for recycling call for a massive redistribution of global energy flows. "Eco-Monitoring and Control Centers" are to be aligned with new networks of strategic planning that transcend traditional political structures in the relentless pursuit of efficient allocation of resources. Efficiency becomes humanity. McHale's conclusions are familiar but the basis of his argument in a highly idiosyncratic, if not fetishistic, understanding of prosthetics has been forgotten, along with the curious role played by architecture in ecological thought.

The pivotal chapter of *The Future of the Future* is entitled "Man Plus," accessorized man. McHale was fascinated by the attachment of artificial limbs. Usually made in response to some kind of human defect (through birth, degenerative disease, or amputation), they can also amplify and diversify the human organism. McHale presents a whole succession of prosthetic attachments as a general model of cultural production and restructuring. The argument starts with crude mechanical hands and ends with the subtle control of machines through body electricity. To accessorize and extend the body is not to simply attach a prosthetic limb or place the body within some prosthetic apparatus. It also means passing that apparatus right into the internal nervous system, letting the machinery of the body interact with the machinery that is outside it to produce a new kind of body. The limit between interior and exterior, organic and technological, gives way. The inevitable consequence is the "extension," as McHale puts it, of the human nervous system into a generalized cybernetic system. Using this explosion of the human nervous system as a model for all technological development, he conceives of technology itself as an organic system. Ecologists would no longer talk about plant life, food chains, mineral resources, atmospheric conditions, and so on. The technological world becomes the new nature, the artificial nature that needs to be analyzed in ecological terms. The prosthetic body grows into a landscape, a terrain that can be occupied. Each successive extension of the body transforms the space it occupies. The distinction between body and space soon collapses. In ecological terms, human flesh is but a transitional event in the continuous redistribution of energy. With the arrival of the artificial body, ecological management is nothing more than the management of hyper-extended flows of nervous energy.

McHale theorizes "extension" in all its forms. He uses the word, for example, to describe the way hallucinogenic drugs transform the nervous system. Likewise, cryogenics, freezing the body immediately after or before death, is understood as an "extension" of life, and therefore the body. It is the last move in the "vertical extension" of the body up into outer space and down into the underwater depths. The body "extends" itself in time, which includes the technologically assisted exploration of history. The future and the past become natural habitats. All these diverse technologies collaborate to produce a "species extension," a fundamental transformation of the morphological and social condition of humanity.

The point of the "Man Plus" chapter is that the accelerated growth of the prosthetically extended body necessarily leads to networks of overlapping technological systems that envelop the planet as a single system. The illustrations gradually pass from traditional prosthetics to images of the international media. Simple mechanical hands give way to more sophisticated hands, then hands detached from the body that operates them, then a body mirrored by robots, which in turn gives way to communications systems: the first fax machine, the first video phones, and so on. Before long, images of radar systems and radio telescopes are presented as enormous ears, which give way to spacecraft—remote sensory systems that fly around the globe. Parts of our body float above and around the planet—eyes, ears, and noses on the loose. The artificial body is globalized into a vast electronic network mirroring the internal electricity of the nervous system. It is one body at the scale of the planet, one ecosystem in which the distinction between culture and nature cannot easily be made. Such an ecology calls for new kinds of resource management. The uneven distribution of resources has to be combated with new tactics. Institutions like the nation state, which interfere with the flows of energy, have to be abandoned. Indeed, politics itself becomes obsolete.

McHale's argument about prosthetics is a social argument. The structure of human interaction changes with the ever-changing structure of the body. The hyper-extended nervous system is also an ecology of ideas. Language, for example, is described as the first prosthesis. It is not surprising that the central issue quickly becomes the latest communication technologies. The contemporary social condition is to be found in the extremes of state-of-the-art technology. Physical technology is understood as social technology. It is not that social life deploys various technologies to sustain itself or that social life can be found within technological space. Rather, social life can only reside in prosthetic accessories. As McHale puts it: "Man is a social animal only through his extensions." Prosthetics are "psycho-physical extensions" of man by which organized human thought covers the globe as a fundamental part of the overall ecological system. McHale speaks about "conceptual extension" as often as he speaks about physical extension. Ideas, like bodies, can be prosthetically transformed and dispersed. Inside the ever larger, interconnected, and entangled network that envelops the planet are layers of concepts that evolve and interact continuously like the weather. It is in this intricate play between organic processes, economies, technologies, and concepts that the nuances of McHale's understanding of ecology lies.

What does this have to do with architecture? Everything. When the German zoologist Ernst Haechel coined the term *ecology* in 1873, he described its etymological sources in the Greek *oikos*—house or household economy—and *logos*—knowledge. Ecology is knowledge of the house, of household economy. From the beginning, ecology is a thinking about domestic space. For McHale, the globe has become a single space, one house: "The home planet has become a minimal conceptual unit of occupancy for the whole human family." Everybody lives in a vast electronic house. Consequently, "the feeling of at home has been mobilized round the planet." Even the sense of belonging to a place has been mobilized. New forms of inhabitation have emerged. To think of ecology is to think of this colossal domestic architecture. McHale's ecological agenda is "planetary housekeeping." The global ecosystem has become a kind of building, an interior, a domestic space that needs to be redesigned. The concluding chapter of *The Ecological Context*, argues that "we need to design our way forward" and symptomatically ends with the claim that we need to establish "what are the ecological or housekeeping rules that govern human occupancy."

To talk about ecology in architecture is not to bring ecological thinking to architecture. Ecology is, from the beginning, a certain kind of thinking about or from architecture. McHale constantly deploys an architectural rhetoric. In fact, *The Future of the Future* was first published in 1967 as *2000+*, a special issue of *Architectural Design* edited by McHale. In the same year, other sections of the book appeared as "World Dwelling," an essay in *Perspecta*, the student journal of the Yale School of Architecture, which was republished in *Towards The Future*, a special issue of *Design Quarterly* edited by McHale. Likewise, *The Ecological Context* is a reprint of one of a series of reports produced between 1963 and 1967 by "The World Resources Inventory," which was founded at the International Union of Architects Congress of 1961 by Buckminster Fuller, who was also fascinated by prosthetics. McHale, who wrote the first monograph on

Fuller, directed the inventory. His thinking is basically a reworking of Fuller's program. Architectural ambitions underpin it at every turn.

The architecture is elusive. There doesn't appear to be any recognizable designs as such in either *The Future of the Future* or in *The Ecological Context*, even though both were published by one of the most important architectural publishers of the day. Yet specific architectural proposals are stitched into the argument. A complete re-thinking of the house takes place between the lines. Specifically, McHale rethinks the relationship between material shelter and the technologies that have redefined the meaning of shelter. A new attitude to architecture surreptitiously emerges from the ecological philosophy. Indeed, a manifesto for the house can be found there. McHale follows Fuller in describing the house as "a rentable fully serviced facility like the telephone." The telephone network becomes the new architectural ideal. The identity of the house is radically displaced. McHale rejects the idea of home ownership and calls for "expendable and expandable" houses. Everything is mobilized. At one moment, the house is described as a portable prosthetic skin and at another the car is described as "a mobile extension of the house." All the accessories of modern life become housing elements. "Car, boat, plane, motel, vacation cabin, trailer, restaurant, theatre, etc., are extended home roofs." Even the space produced by projections and drugs is embraced. All that is left of the traditional house is a "services pack" that can go anywhere, "a dwelling services unit which will operate with equal facility in the earth or on the moon." The space suit becomes a model home. And just as the house is mobilized and heads out into the world, the world comes into the house through all the new communication technologies. At most, the physical house is but the "home base" in a network: "The home hearth concept has become detached from the material paraphernalia of dwellings." Prosthetics at once consolidate and disperse the house. Architecture restlessly circulates. It flows.

Again, this is not just the application of ecological arguments about technology to the specific technology of the house. It is the ongoing extension of the house that has produced the idea of a single ecosystem whose flows can be managed with new ecological principles. The globalization of the house makes a globalizing theory possible: one house, one theory.

The basis of the argument can be found earlier in McHale's career. While he published his first promotional article on Buckminster Fuller in a 1956 issue of *Architecture Design*, his particular attraction to architecture only became clear a year later when he did the cover for "Machine made America," a special issue of the same journal. He presented an artificial body made up of a collage of images that "reflects the world of infra-grilled steak, premixed cake, dream kitchens, dream cars, machine tools, power mixers, parkways, ticket tapes, sparkplugs and electronics." The image was followed by two pages of "Marginalia" that linked popular culture to architectural culture. There are images of houses built from catalogs, loudspeaker designs by architects, Fuller domes, car styling, push button automatic transmissions, office desks with push-button panels for lighting and temperature, waste and TV controls, dream houses, mechanical beds, rotisseries for sunbathers, highway interchanges, and so on. McHale's self-portrait at the top of the article shows his face alongside a robotic head described as his "spare head." Architecture is united to popular culture by way of the new artificial body.

McHale was an artist at the time and was devoted to the robotic body, as can be seen in numerous photograms and collages of the 1950s that evolved seamlessly into a fascination with popular culture and then architecture. Since 1954, McHale, along with Lawrence Alloway, was the convenor of The Independent Group pivotal discussions at the Institute of Contemporary Art in London, a role he had taken over from the budding architectural historian Reyner Banham. The bond between prosthetics and architecture became even more explicit in a 1957 essay entitled "Technology in the Home." It begins by announcing that "technological changes in the home have accelerated in the post-war years, keeping pace in this with the home extensions—like the automobile, the Espresso café, the Wimpey bar, the movies—and even the pub." The internal and external extension of the home has occurred without help of architects. The appeal to popular culture is an appeal to a newly emerging architecture for the prosthetically extended human body that the formal discipline of architecture cannot comprehend. McHale insists that "where the penetration of the home by technology has occurred to the greatest degree, i.e., the kitchen, the architect's part has come down to providing a roof for a completely 'packaged' mechanical utility." The architect merely provides the package for the package. Unsurprisingly, Fuller is immediately identified as the one architect who has been able to extend the limits of the discipline through a series of house designs developed "outside of standard architectural practice."

The transformation of the house is inseparable from the transformation of popular culture. In 1959, McHale published the two parts of an article called "The Expendable Icon" in successive issues of *Architectural Design*. He insists that the rise of "environment extensions" in the form of the media have "pushed man's frontiers almost to the stars." The article examines the economy of popular images in an age in which "the whole range of the sensory spectrum has been extended—man can see more, hear more, travel faster—experience more than ever before." While McHale beings by announcing, "Architects and designers are professionally concerned with communicating visually and, where not actively engaged, we are all participants in the process of mass-communications," the only explicit reference to architecture is the inclusion of cathedrals in the list of the old forms of stable imagery that have been displaced by the new media. The point was not elaborated until "The Plastic Parthenon," a 1961 talk by McHale at the ICA, which explored the way plastic replicas of architectural monuments have acquired more cultural significance than the monuments they replicate. A new architectural space is constructed within the accelerated flow of substitute images: "Besides the enlargement of the *physical* world now available to our direct experience, these media virtually extend our physical environment, providing a constant stream of moving, fleeting images of the world for our daily appraisal. They provide psychical mobility for the greater mass of our citizens. Through these devices we can telescope time, move through history and span the world in a great variety of unprecedented ways." Buildings have long succumbed to this new ecology. The "machine aesthetic" of modern architecture is described as never more than an aesthetic, an "image of functional modernity rather than its actuality," an image that circulated the globe in an unprecedented way before giving way to other images.

The point had already been made by Banham three years earlier. Modern architecture, which explicitly described itself as a prosthetic technology, was just an image—an image of prosthetics rather than a form of prosthetics. For Banham, Fuller was a refreshing exception. In fact, McHale had invited Fuller to give a lecture at the ICA in June 1958 called "Man Plus." The Independent Group's longstanding fascination with artificial bodies interacted with that of the architect. Banham shared Fuller's mission to produce a truly prosthetic architecture that would at the same time engage the ever exploding culture of images—hence his simultaneous commitment to the state-of-the-art in technology and the state-of-the-art in styling. In the attempt to get beyond an image of prosthetics to the prosthetic technology itself, the Independent Group didn't abandon the image as such. On the contrary, it was obsessed with the prosthetic structure of images in popular culture.

McHale elaborated this obsession into a prolonged discourse about ecology. It was precisely when he was finishing his book on Fuller that he offered the plastic pop simulation of the Parthenon, along with reconstructions of the Taj Mahal in Los Angeles and Medieval castles at Disneyland, as the paradigm of the new ecology of images. The "cyclical mobility" of images through space and time is aligned with the reconfiguration of architecture on ecological principles. Simulation is understood as a means of species survival. The expendability of images is directly linked to the seeming non-expendability of the body. The capacity to use, re-use, and discard images is seen as the means to survive new environments and new time frames. Images are literally consumed as a form of nutrition. Prosthetic extension is a form of ingestion. As the body expands, the environment is literally brought inside. Space gets reconstituted. Architecture is what you swallow. Even the Gothic cathedral succumbs to its own reproduction in digital archives. The traditional paradigm of the inescapable presence of an auratic object, the immediate, uncontrollable, unforgettable, irreproducible experience of a place is simply absorbed: "Most of Europe's main cathedrals, if destroyed, may now be reconstructed from the detailed photogramatic records." Architectural experience is recycled. The "authentic" experience becomes no less an image than its simulations. Furthermore, recycling allows the same materials to be transformed from one object to another, such that the materials "move," as McHale puts it, through culture. Material is morphed through space and time. Culture becomes nothing more than the organization of such flows. Architectural culture is but a rhythmic ecology of images, even if those images are not simply visual. Architecture becomes plastic, in the sense of a morphing communication system that restlessly circulates around the planet. Defining space within flows, it is an artificial nature inhabited on an everyday basis.

The expendable image circulating through popular culture becomes a model for an ecology of resources. While "human consciousness has expanded electronically," McHale insists that it has done so precisely to oppose the "economics of scarcity." He did not abandon the pop images of his early years for the statistical analyses of science and ecology. On the contrary, his introduction to 2000+ suggests, "The imagery of technology may be as powerful an agency of change as the rational understanding of a scientific and technological basis." He is attracted to Fuller precisely because he is first and foremost an "image maker." Ecology is a question of images in the end, images of architecture and the architecture of images.

Such images are rarely innocent. McHale and Fuller's fantasy of a post-political house preserves the fantasy of the happy family. The production of a single global house can only be understood as the eradication of all military and political conflict if violence is understood as something that occurs between houses rather than within them. But the very idea of the house is structured by violence, whether physical, emotional, conceptual, or ideological. If ecology is knowledge of the house—architectural knowledge—it should also be knowledge of this structural violence. After all, the "natural" ecosystem is spectacularly brutal. Ecological design must rethink the house rather than simply recirculate a generic suspect image. It is not that McHale simply ignores the politics of the house:

effacement, entrapment, ritualistic brutality, closets, and so on. On the contrary, he unwittingly exercised it.

At the same time, it is important to note that while fundamental inequities in the formation of the house can be addressed, there can be no such thing as the politically correct house. The very idea of the house is premised on violence, which takes the most obvious forms but also subtle ones that are perhaps the most lethal in the end. It is not just a matter of finding a better image for the house. Furthermore, the actual design of houses has an extremely complicated relationship to the institutional function of the image of the house. It is all too easy to underestimate the complexity of the relationship between what it is to design or even talk about a house and the sense in which we always inhabit certain images of houses whose consequences we cannot face—to such an extent that it is actually the way we avoid them that produces the sense of "at home." To inhabit a house is usually to suppress its nightmares. These complications have always organized architectural discourse but it becomes increasingly difficult to neglect them, since our houses, the everyday spaces we inhabit, are increasingly defined by images. It becomes increasingly obvious that architecture is literally carved into the flow of images. Ecological theories of flow are more useful to the architect than ever before. Recycling will inevitably be recycled.

This will require care. The overt politics of ecology—the equitable management of resources—almost always preserves certain regressive ideological formations. The essentially imperialistic and patronizing structure of most ecological discourse never distributes resources equitably. Perhaps architectural discourse can help in monitoring this regressive tendency. Rather than simply reapplying ecological discourse to design, some of the perennial enigmas of the house that architects explore could be used to rethink ecology. The discourse can be rewired.

Mark Wigley is a Professor of Architectural History and Theory at Princeton University. He is the author of The Architecture of Deconstruction: Derrida's Haunt *(1993),* White Walls, Designer Dresses: The Fashioning of Modern Architecture *(1995), and* Constant's New Babylon: The Hyper-Architecture of Desire *(1998).*

ately interpret them into built environment. Recurrent theme in SPACE COMIC universe is mobile computer "BRAIN" and flexing tentacles

MONTHS PASS... AND AS THE DYING SUN CAUSES THE EARTH TO FREEZE, MANKIND DIGS DEEPER AND DEEPER BENEATH THE SURFACE...

WE ARE DOWN FAR ENOUGH! THERE IS SUFFICIENT WARMTH HERE TO KEEP OUR PEOPLE ALIVE FOR GENERATIONS!

I SUCCEEDED IN SC... UP THE "BRAIN". ALL... NOW IT'S TURNED T... MACHINE AGAINST I... MASTERS! GOT TO T... SAVE THEM!

KKLLIKK

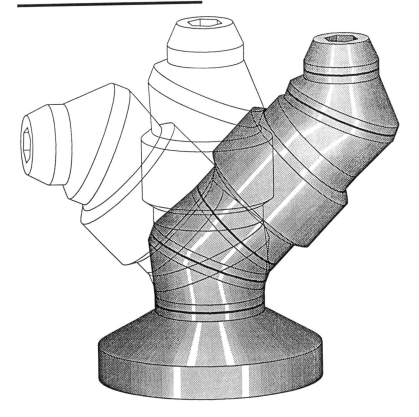

The Persistence of Industrial Memory[1]

Mark Dery

Vaporware

Not all that is solid melts into air. Our cultural landscape is strewn with the semiotic flotsam of the Machine Age—cold, hard reminders of the persistence of industrial memory in what is supposed to be an information society.

The mechanical paradigm is very much with us, although one would never know it from the prevailing rhetoric of etherealization, from Bryan Fawcett's "deliberation on the disappearance of the world" into the vortex of simulation in *The Public Eye* to O.B. Hardison's *Disappearing Through the Skylight*, a technodeterminist overview of the twentieth century. Hardison's root metaphor for the effects of technological progress on industrial modernity is disappearance, most notably the disappearance of the very notion of what it means to be human in a terminal culture that is ever more invasive (pacemakers, cochlear implants, artificial kidneys, prosthetic limbs), extrusive (videoconferencing, electronic bulletin boards), and immersive (computer games, theme park simulation rides, mall virtual reality).

Another variation on the theme of dematerialization surfaces in the special effects—images of implosion, scatteration, and so forth—that have turned postmodern theory into a subgenre of science fiction: Fredric Jameson's dizzy, centrifugal evocation in *Postmodernism* of the "fragmented and schizophrenic decenter-

Robotic assembler arm, approximately 4,000,000 atoms without base (K. Eric Drexler, Nanosystems, John Wiley, 1992).

ing and dispersion" of the self in postmodern culture; Arthur Kroker's hebephrenic rhapsodies, in the *Panic Encyclopedia*, about the "fin-de-millennium" imploding "under the twin pressures of the ecstacy of catastrophe and the anxiety of fear," the "dissolution of facts into the flash of thermonuclear cultural 'events' in the postmodern situation."[2]

The rhetoric of etherealization isn't all cant, of course. Few would deny that factory capitalism has been superseded in America by an information economy characterized by what Buckminster Fuller called the "ephemeralization of work"—the reduction of labor to the manipulation on computers of symbols that stand in for the manufacturing process. It is a commonplace, too, that the engines of industrial production have yielded to a phantasmagoric capitalism that produces intangible commodities—Hollywood blockbusters, TV programs, high-tech theme parks, one-minute megatrends, financial transactions that flicker through fiber-optic bundles to computer terminals a world away. "Only 17 percent of working Americans now manufacture anything, down from 22 percent as recently as 1980," wrote Robert B. Reich in a 1992 *New York Times* essay.[3] According to a recent *Times* article, American films generate the second largest trade surplus of any American industry.[4] Immaterial commodities dominate the domestic market as well: according to a 1994 *Business Week* report, "entertainment and recreation (not health care or autos) have provided the biggest boost to consumer spending" since 1991.[5] We are moving from an age of hardware into what might be called an age of vaporware. ("Vaporware" is compu-slang for "[p]roducts announced far in advance of any release [which may or may not actually take place] according to *The New Hacker's Dictionary*.[6] I use the term metaphorically, to refer to the increasingly wraithlike nature of digital culture at the end of the twentieth century.)

Our ethereal economy has a cultural fallout. In a world where the "traffic in 'information' and abstract value (credit, junk bonds, and so forth) has accelerated beyond the economy of material goods," writes Stuart Ewen, "anorectic female bodies aestheticize the ethic of nothingness. Black stereo receivers fade into the darkness of the woodwork, while their digital readouts sanctify a society more and more dazzled by the play of light."[7] The rhetoric of etherealization reaches its apotheosis in science fiction visions of the infosphere as a Radiant City drawn in frozen light—the eerie, incandescent otherworld of William Gibson's cyberspace, where computer memory is crystallized in "[l]ines of light ranged in the nonspace of the mind, clusters and constellations of data."[8] As we spend ever greater portions of our lives immersed in electronic entertainment, communication, and financial transactions, the mundane world begins to assume an air of unreality.

This reversal manifests itself in an advertisement for the latest generation of Intel microprocessors: a brightly lit metropolitan nightscape in which gleaming avenues link a cluster of downtown skyscrapers and a cozy tract home in the suburbs reveals itself, at a second glance, to be part of a circuit board. The smaller structures are electronic components; the "avenues" are circuits, radiating out from the Intel processor that powers the "city." In a very real sense, Intel implies, we live not in the urban centers or "edge cities" to which we commute but in the data-spaces inside our computers. "The city of the future," writes the architectural theorist Mark Taylor, "is a simulated city."[9]

Through the Rear-View Mirror, Darkly

The etherealization of culture and technology is writ large in "Ten Points, Ten Examples," Bernard Tschumi's reading of architectural history as a "continuing transformation of buildings . . . from material to immaterial . . . from the heavy stones of the Egyptians to Roman vaults, then Gothic arches, then iron construction, the curtain wall, structural glass, immaterial light screens, Albert Speer's Cathedral of Light, holograms, and now virtual reality."[10] In like fashion, the countervailing mechanical paradigm—industrial memories that persist because, rather than in spite, of this etherealization—is ubiquitous in architecture's phantom double, set design, and throughout popular culture, in graphic and industrial design.

A brutalist aesthetic percolated into mass culture in the early '90s, manifesting itself in *The Party Machine*, a TV discotheque in which mini-skirted, midriffed models gyrated suggestively in front of giant cogwheels and convoluted tubing. Soon, it seemed, the new brutalism was everywhere: in music videos, dancers stalked catwalks, past designer blast furnaces reminiscent of the factory in

Metropolis. The soundtrack was fittingly mechanical: Jimmy Jam and Terry Lewis's New Jack Swing echoed with metallic cling-clangs, hammered out by inhumanly precise drum machines.

Industrial dance bands also harked back to the Machine Age, playing a brutalist music characterized by pile-driver rhythms and the sampled pandemonium of heavy industry and the big city. Industrial beat music used angst-ridden vocals hemmed in by machines as a metonymy for the human condition in cyberculture. Produced with an arsenal of synthesizers, sequencers, and samplers, it was troubled, ironically, by repression through technology. But while the sound of industrial machinery signified microminiaturized technologies multiplying all around us, the image of hulking machinery, in record cover art and promo photos, embodied masculinist values of brute force and steely toughness.

The return of the repressed machine is staged, as well, in the bruising, bolted-together mise-en-scenes of film and tv. In Hollywood movies, we see the Machine Age revenant in the vaguely panoptical prison-cum-cloister-cum-ore refinery in *Alien III* (1992), *The Hudsucker Proxy* (1994), *The Shadow* (1994), and even in the *Star Trek: The Next Generation* spinoff *Deep Space Nine*, where the high-tech elevator doors of the earlier series have devolved into outsized cogwheels moved by locomotive drivers.

But it is the *Batman* movies that epitomize Machine Age redux. Set in the Gotham City Albert Speer would have designed if he were alive and well and working for Michael Eisner, *Batman* (1989) is steeped in a retro-futurist aesthetic that the film's production designer Anton Furst characterized, in a postmodernist one-liner, as "a period view of the future."[11] Inspired in part by Shin Takamatsu's 1983 Kyoto dental surgery, *Batman*'s Flugelheim Museum is a hodgepodge of Brutalism, brownstone arches, and 1930s motifs; its rivet-studded steel facade conjures an Art Deco power station on steroids. Invoking the macho modernism of Louis Sullivan, Italian Futurism, and, tellingly, Albert Speer, Furst's Gotham is at once a resurrection of the Machine Age in all its brawny glory and a grim cenotaph to its rusty memory.

Why, at a time when cultural commentators are directing our attention to the vertiginous speedup of the industrial into the post-industrial, is the psychic landscape of the mass imagination littered with dynamos and foundries, Art Deco, and Fascist architecture? McLuhan's theory of "rear-view mirrorism" in *The Medium is the Message* offers one explanation: namely "When faced with a totally new situation, we tend always to attach ourselves to the objects, to the flavor of the most recent past.... We look at the present through a rear-view mirror. We march backwards into the future."[12] He elaborates on this notion in a 1969 *Playboy* interview, asserting that "an environment becomes fully visible only when it has been superseded by a new environment."[13] Narrative concerns aside, the underlying reason for *Batman*'s "period view of the future," McLuhan would argue, is that we are "benumbed" by any new technology and therefore "tend to make the old environment more visible." We do so, he argues, by aestheticizing the old environment, "just as ... we're now doing with the garbage of the mechanical environment via pop art."[14]

But McLuhan failed to consider the obvious—namely, that the pop artists of his day were using the "garbage of the mechanical environment" to tell stories about the emerging electronic age. Contemporary industrial art such as metal machine music, the robotic spectacles of San Francisco's Survival Research Laboratories, and the cyborgian performance art of the Phoenix, Arizona-based Comfort/Control uses mechanical iconography as an paradoxical metaphor for an information society whose technological totem, the computer, resists representation. Sealed in a smooth, inscrutable shell, the computer's inner workings are too complex, too changeable for the imagination to gain purchase on them; only when it is imaged in the heavy metal of the Machine Age can this post-industrial engine be grasped. The tiny "embedded microprocessors that help run everything from cars to coffee makers to airliners are even more widespread than personal computers, but they are largely invisible to the casual viewer," notes the cultural critic Gary Chapman. "Many people probably have a vague idea that there is a computer under the hood of the newer model automobiles, and that it helps run the engine. But how the computer does this, where it is, and how it can malfunction are typically mysteries for most people."[15]

The recrudescence of the mechanical paradigm returns us to the Industrial Revolution in a sociopolitical as well as a semiotic sense. The new brutalism mirrors the rise of a neo-Dickensian America characterized by an increasingly polarized, two-tiered society "with an upper tier of high-wage skilled workers and an increasing 'underclass' of low-paid labor" and the unemployed, in the words of a special commission headed by former Labor Secretary John T. Dunlop.[16]

On a psychological level, the persistence of industrial memory betokens what Samuel Delany has called a yearning for "a world where the girders show." Incomprehensible and intangible, the information society is shot through with the longing for an explicable, touchable technoculture (even if an oppressive one). In this light, technology and the built environment are "humanized" by the ravages of time; the decaying remains of broken-down machines and derelict factories are industrial memento mori, metaphorically inviting us to contemplate our own mortality. Decrepitude strips machines of their symbolic status as emblems of the superhuman and casts them into the organic world. Falling apart and gnawed by rust, they resemble rotten logs overgrown by mold; in a sense, they have returned to nature, or at least Second Nature, in the same way that Gothic ruins were seen as a metaphor for nature by Romantic poets and painters. Our anxiety over the posthuman supremacy of our ever-smaller, ever-smarter technologies has invested the corroded skeletons of the Machine Age with the same sublime sadness and poetic mystery that William Wordsworth and Charles T. Turner found in the ruins of Tintern Abbey.

Obsolescence and decay draw an aesthetic veil between us and our tools; by virtue of its uselessness, archaic tech attains the status of art. In his essay, "Urban Gothic," the Los Angeles artist Mike Kelley writes, "I live in a warehouse district downtown. It is populated by artists now that the businesses have all dried up. From the picture window in my loft can be seen the skeletal remains of once-thriving factories. . . . Since the structures are no longer functioning, they have slipped into my territory, the realm of non-functionality, the world of aesthetics."[17]

In a neat parallel to the eighteenth century vogue among English garden designers for faux Gothic ruins, a retro-tech fad hallmarked by the decorative use of industrial motifs has left its mark on contemporary architecture and interior design. According to the urban theorist Mike Davis, "most of the restaurants and bookstores and micro-breweries on [L.A.'s] West side have some kind of decor that has to do with industrialization—[it's] a Second Machine Age. People whose daily work has almost nothing to do anymore with the worldly production of goods seem to desire huge gears and obsolete machinery."[18]

Armageddon Dildos[19]

The evanescence of postmodern technology has profound implications for the American male, whose mythic birthright throughout this century has included a St. Francis of Assisi-like dominion over the machine kingdom, typically manifested in a mastery of intractable gadgets. The conversion from a manufacturing economy to an information society and the supersession of penetrable mechanical devices by hermetic digital ones challenges the masculinity of men who use mechanical know-how or heavy-duty hardware, be it tool or toy, to signify their maleness. This challenge dovetails with the larger crisis of masculinity brought on by automation, downsizing, and the erosion of traditional gender roles.

In the movie *Terminator 2: Judgement Day* (1991), uneasiness over the displacement of industrial culture and the dissolution of conventional definitions of masculinity erupt in a titanic struggle between hardware and vaporware. A cautionary tale about a society that leaves its technology on automatic pilot, *T2* is also a curiously reactionary morality play about our passage from an age of industrial manufacturing into one of symbol-manipulating. Beset by anxieties over the liquid indeterminacy of cyberculture, the movie clings tenaciously to the comfortingly "masculine" solidity of heavy industry (a singular irony in a film so dependent on digital trickery). The T-800 Schwarzenegger Terminator stands in for the dark, satanic mills of the Rust Belt which, once menacing, now seem reassuringly familiar in contrast to the disconcertingly fluid future promised by Silicon Valley. That future is bodied forth in the T-1000 Terminator—an "advanced prototype" made of "mimetic polyalloy" that assumes the appearance of "anything it samples by physical contact." Liquefying into a featureless silver mannequin, it hardens into a flawless copy of anyone, or anything, it has touched.

In the cosmology of *T2*, the computer is the root of all evil, from the malevolent SkyNet, a SDI-like computerized defense system that acquires sentience and rebels against its human creators, a la Frankenstein; to the PCs of the computer scientist destined to create SkyNet, their hard drives crammed with forbidden knowledge; to the fateful CPU chip (a blueprint for a Terminator) that is consigned to the lake of fire at the movie's end; to the T-1000 itself, the uncanny incarnation of a cyberculture characterized by the dematerialization, via digitization, of labor, commodities, even the genetic code of living organisms. Miniaturized and nearly noiseless, its unfathomable mechanisms swallowed up in sleek, sensuous casings, electronic technology looks unavoidably "feminine" alongside the gargantuan, clanking brutes of the Machine Age, their camshafts and cogwheels exposed for all to see. In her essay "Muscular Circuitry: The Invincible Armored Cyborg in Cinema," Claudia Springer transposes the terms traditionally assigned to the reproductive organs of each sex to information and industrial technologies. The female genitalia, "hidden, internal, and inert," are identified with "fluid and fluctuating internal systems," while the male organs, "forceful and agressive," are associated with industrial machinery.[20]

Springer contends that unlike industrial machinery, "electronic technology functions quietly and passively, and yet industrial-age metaphors for representing technology persist in the Information Age."[21] T2's rear-view mirrorism perpetuates 19th century "notions of technology, sexual difference, and gender roles," she argues, "in order to resist the transformations brought about by the new postmodern social order." Thus, T2's demonization of information machines and veneration of monster Harleys, seven-chamber grenade launchers, and, first and foremost, the T-800 itself, can be seen as a masculine recoil from what Springer calls the "feminization of electronic technology." She concludes, "What aggressive, muscular cyborg imagery does is assert the dominance of a phallic metaphor for technology. . . . The cyborg rampages across the screen as if to deny that there has been a feminization of late twentieth-century technology."[22]

There is, to put it oxymoronically, a giddy dysphoria to our historical moment—a vertigo induced, perhaps, by the notion that even we will one day disintegrate into so many zeroes and ones. The Human Genome Project reminds us, disconcertingly, that a human being is "little more than a cloud of information," to borrow the critic Thomas Hine's memorable phrase.[23] The artificial intelligence researcher Hans Moravec has theorized the transmigration of human consciousness into cyberspace; mapped onto computer memory by a theoretical process called "downloading," a disembodied mind would live forever, perhaps as a discarnate inhabitant of one of Mark Taylor's simulated cities.

It can hardly be happenstance that one of the totemic samples of early techno music is the phrase "Pure Energy," spoken by *Star Trek*'s Mister Spock, just as it is no coincidence that the climax of the virtual reality fable *Lawnmower Man* comes when the protagonist declares, "I'm going to . . . complete the final stage of my evolution. I'm going to project myself into the mainframe computer; I'll become pure energy." Fearful that we will be dematerialized in a swirl of glittering data-bits, like passengers in a *Star Trek* transporter, we cling desperately to the bulkheads and boilerplate of a somehow more reassuring brutality.

Postscript from the Future: Soft Machines for Living

Even as the T-1000 puts a protean face on popular anxieties about the accelerating speed and shifting shape of digital culture, it embodies a biomorphic aesthetic consonant with the "neo-biological" paradigm theorized by Kevin Kelly, *Wired*'s executive editor and resident cyber-rhapsodist.

In *Out of Control: The Rise of Neo-Biological Civilization*, Kelly argues that "the realm of the born—all that is nature—and the realm of the *made*—all that is humanly constructed—are becoming one. Machines are becoming biological and the biological is becoming engineered."[24] The modernist vision of a rationalist, functionalist future wrought in "gray steel" is being superseded, he maintains, by what might be called a "meme-splice" of technosphere and biosphere. Kelly's cybernetic ecology is composed of self-replicating, self-repairing machines whose integration of metaphors drawn from nature (the sociobiology of beehives and ant colonies, the mechanics of bird flocking and insect locomotion) will theoretically enable them to adapt, learn, and evolve. "The hallmark of the industrial age has been its exaltation of mechanical design," writes Kelly. "The hallmark of a neo-biological civilization is that it returns the designs of its creations toward the organic, again."[25]

Kelly invokes evolutionary theory and chaos science to legitimate laissez-faire cybercapitalism—a "network economy" of decentralized, outsourced "economic superorganisms," able to adapt to the nonlinear dynamics of the global economic ecosystem. Going further, he writes swooningly of the "new spiritualism" destined to flow from network economics, the emergent "global mind," soon to be born of our electronic interconnectedness. His New Age cyber-raptures sound suspiciously like a Vulcan mind-meld between Teilhard de Chardin and George Gilder: noetic Reaganomics.[26]

Nonetheless, there's no denying Kelly's assertion that "engineered biology and biotechnology will eclipse the importance of mechanical technology": the current proliferation of biological and evolutionary metaphors, from Kelly's "neo-biology" to the zoologist Richard Dawkins's "meme" (a highly contagious information pattern that infests a culture by leaping from one host mind to another in almost viral fashion), signals the growing influence of biotechnology and genetic engineering, the flagship technologies of the next millennium.

These megatrends are poetically reflected in the return of streamlining in upscale consumer electronics (the undulating curves of the Epson PhotoPC Digital Camera), exercise gear (the gladiatorial Deco of Oxygen's rollerblades), office furniture (the Eames noir of the Aeron Chair), and, most obviously, automobile design (the rippling flanks of the Saturn sl2, the pneumatic post-moderne of the Dodge Neon, the intrauterine interior of the Toyota Camry). Their gently swelling contours suggestive of flexed muscle, the new breed of biomorphic commodities makes semiotic sense in a culture beguiled—and bedeviled—by the cyborgian promise of biotechnology, genetic engineering, artificial life, artificial intelligence, bionic medicine, and nanotechnology.

Moreover, *terminal inertia*—going nowhere at the speed of light via technologies that enable us to overfly virtual landscapes while standing still—is standard operating procedure for an ever expanding segment of the high-tech society, from Robert Reich's "symbolic analysts" (scientists, software developers, engineers, architects, and others who manipulate information for a living) to low-wage data-entry workers. As growing num-

Green Building, a proposal by Future Systems for an office building. London, 1990.

bers of us come to rest in ergonomic workstations, we are increasingly extending our sedentary bodies through media prostheses—McLuhan's "extensions of man." There is poetic significance in the fact that more and more of our tools are assuming organic contours at a time when we are retrofitting and refunctioning ourselves to facilitate the seamless interface of mind and meat with an increasingly wired world.

Charles Jencks has used the term "organi-tech" to describe the architectural manifestation of the neo-biological aesthetic. In *The Architecture of the Jumping Universe: How Complexity Science is Changing Architecture and Culture,* he spades up the roots of organicism in architecture, from Frank Lloyd Wright's call for an organic architecture to the work of Hugo Haring, perched perilously "on the edge of modernism," to its minor role in the "humanist" architecture of Alvar Aalto, to the pullulating, overgrown ornamentation of Art Nouveau, which attains its apotheosis in the hothouse muta-tions of Antonio Gaudi. According to Jencks, the biomorphic has been marginalized throughout architectural history: "Curves, undu-lations, and natural forms were mostly confined to ashtrays, door-knobs, and an occasional acoustic form, where they could be justi-fied rationally and economically."[27] In cyberculture, however, modernist architecture's aesthetics of "reductivism, mechanism, and functional determinism" is gradually being undermined by the cultural dynamics of the Information Age, together with the cur-rents identified by Jencks: the new life sciences of chaos and com-plexity, the mainstreaming of the ecology movement, and, on the level of structural engineering, the ability to build curved forms made possible by automated production and new materials.

In the work of Santiago Calatrava, Renzo Piano, and Nicholas Grimshaw, Jencks catches dim glimpses of an "organi-tech" archi-tecture informed by the wondrous strangeness of chaos and com-plexity, and by the computer, which can evolve artificial life forms that feed, breed, die, and decay. "Technology and the utilitarian concerns still predominate over nature and the organic," writes Jencks, but we are loitering at the threshold of a cyborgian archi-tecture that would graft biomorphic elements onto its "regularity and rationality." Calatrava buildings such as the Lyons-Satolas train station in Lyons, France mimic "the tensed, moving body of an ani-mal" and resound with visual echoes of skeletal structures, such as ribs and vertebrae. Piano's Kansai International Airport terminal in Osaka Bay, Japan, is equal parts swooping glider and sleeping bird, the dizzy sweep of its roof punctuated by "bonelike triangular struts" that give the impression of "stacked, parallel dinosaur ribs." Seen from within its glass-skinned, serpentine interior, each of whose 1,728 self-similar glass panes and their stabilizing fins were calculated by computer to be ever so slightly different, Grimshaw's Waterloo terminal for the Channel Tunnel presents "a real image of a twisting, snakelike architecture, close to nature . . . a recog-nized masterpiece of organi-tech, the first building that can be compared to Gaudian architecture without apology. It uses struc-ture as a changing, oppositional set of systems. They fly about in a ballet of give and take, the very image of living form."[28]

Yet, for all its mimesis, Jencks's "organi-tech" remains an architecture of metaphor, like Marcos Novak's vision of a protean virtual architecture. Jencks holds up Frank Gehry as an exemplar who has "[dropped] his commitment to the technological imperative and [embraced] a more fluid architecture."[29] But when will Gehry's "metallic flower"—the rotunda of his design for the new Guggenheim Museum in Bilbao, Spain—bloom in truth, its solar-panel petals opening to greet the sun, its organic metaphor brought to life by microscopic nanomachines that juggle atoms to make the museum grow rooms or sprout a profusion of mushroom-like ventilator chimneys, all at the speed of time-lapse photography? "In the nanotech world, dwellings . . . can be 'grown,' and everything that is manufactured is closer to flesh than stone," predicts Terence McKenna, writing in the future present.[30]

Living buildings conjured out of thin air by teeming, unseen nanomachines are a high-tech realization of Rudolf Doernach's back-to-nature "biotecture," a granola-fueled vision of "self-growing, energy-harvesting, air-delivered biotectonic plant shelters" featured in a 1989 issue of *The Whole Earth Review*. "Non-living architecture is an evolutionary mistake—parasitic, formalistic, non-productive, and anti-biotic," writes Doernach. "My research . . . shows that [a] living, productive plant habitat is possible."[31] The accompanying photos show Doernach's "vegetal houses" in various stages of construction including shaggy wigwams that look like environmentally friendly bunkers for eco-terrorists. In *Out of Control*, Kelly crossbreeds Doernach's "biotecture" with the interactive "House of the Future" from General Electric's "Carousel of Progress" at Disneyland. He imagines "a human-made forest of planted homes and organic churches," each a living building that would "thicken its hide on the side where the wind blows most or rearrange its interior as its inhabitants shifted their use of it," part of a larger architectural ecology that "adapted and flexed and evolved as living creatures do" through the agency of "adaptive technologies, distributed networks, and synthetic evolution."[32]

Gibson's novel *Idoru* offers an unsettling premonition of Kelly's arboreal architecture. In 21st century Tokyo, buildings are spun from nothingness by nanomachines. A character recalls the city's resurrection, after a cataclysmic quake, when "you could see those towers growing, at night. Rooms up top like a honeycomb, and walls just sealing themselves over, one after another . . . like watching a candle melt, but in reverse. That's too scary. Doesn't make a sound. Machines too small to see." Gibson evokes the queasy marvel of restless architecture that shifts with "the sequential contraction of some sea creature's palps."[33] Meanwhile, scientists have already laid the cornerstone for "organi-tech" industrial materials: "biomimetic" polymer gels capable of changing their size or shape in response to stimuli such as acids and bases, thereby converting chemical energy into mechanical activity, like living muscles. Polymer scientists' interest in a softer, wetter technology evinces a shift away from the mechanistic paradigms of the industrial age. According to researcher Yoshihito Osada, growing numbers of scientists are drawing inspiration from "biological systems" such as the sea cucumber, a waterlogged gel stuffed with primitive organs that can nonetheless feed, reproduce, and even defend itself from predators. When threatened, the cucumber dissolves part of its body wall into a viscous mass, making it difficult to grasp. "We believe that in the not too distant future," write Osada and researcher Simon B. Ross-Murphy, "we will find a way to build 'soft' machines that can respond in an intelligent fashion to their environments."[34] Osada has already created squishy blobs that jitter like possessed Jell-O and "gel loopers" that hump along, inchwormlike, when electrified. Surely, the self-morphing smart house—an "advanced prototype" made of "mimetic polyalloy"— cannot be far off.[35]

At the outer bound of scientific possibility, the conjunction of genetic engineering, nanotechnology, and "biochips"—theoretical interfaces between integrated circuits and peripheral nerve axons, based on experiments with brain cells grown on microchips—could beget a living architecture in the literal sense. Of course, in the economy of metaphor, buildings and bodies have always been fungible: the historian of religion Mircea Eliade reminds us that the house-body homology appeared at the dawn of civilization, in archaic religions. And the association of buildings with beings, in Freudian dream analysis, has become a pop-psych staple (exploited, to chilling effect, in *The Amityville Horror*, *The Shining*, and other horror movies about hellhouses, all of them descendants of Edgar Allen Poe's *House of Usher*, with its "vacant eye-like windows").

In architectural discourse, the correlation of architecture and human anatomy, particularly the male body, has been a keynote, from Vitruvius's exhortation in *The Ten Books on Architecture* that the design of a temple emulate the cosmic symetry of a "well-shaped man" to McLuhan's technodeterministic theory that "housing as shelter is an extension of our bodily heat-control mechanisms—a collective skin or garment."[36] Predictably, this tendency reaches its crescendo in odes to the modernist sublime, such as Louis Sullivan's testosterone-soaked description of one of the Marshall Field Company's warehouses as "a man that walks on two legs instead of four, has active muscles . . . lives and breathes . . . in a world of barren pettiness, a male."[37]

Information technologies, as Claudia Springer has noted, reverse the symbolic polarities of industrial modernism, supplanting its technophallic machismo with the "feminine" semiotics of cyberculture: polymorphous, mercurial, ever more miniaturized, and above all biomorphic. (This is not to say, as has been suggested by New Age futurists such as John Perry Barlow or digital Deleuzeans such as Sadie Plant, that the information society is accordingly more "feminine," and therefore more feminist, than the age of heavy industry; only that the visual grammar and internal logic of cyberculture exhibit characteristics historically associated with femaleness.)

There is poetic justice in sci-fi visions of the literalization of such metaphors, through biotechnology and nanotechnology, in organi-tech buildings fashioned from flesh and blood. In unwitting mockery of Sullivan's he-man warehouse, Kitsune—the Brobdingnagian "Wallmother" in Bruce Sterling's cyberpunk opus *Schismatrix*—not only lives and breathes but literally contains multitudes. Her bioengineered flesh has been fashioned into a cavernous space, measureless to man, within which people live and work to the accompaniment of "a steady rushing of arteries and an occasional bowel-like gurgle from the naked walls."[38] Sterling's delirious descriptions of her are a *Fantastic Voyage* through a giant Venus of Willendorf: "The room was full of flesh. It was made of it: satiny brown skin, broken here and there by rugs of lustrous black hair and mauve flashes of mucus membrane."[39] Kitsune's walls literally have ears, and eyes as well, and her biomass contains still smaller buildings, "the sleek pink of [their] sphinctered doors sliding imperceptibly into skin lightly stippled with down."[40] She's a genetically engineered sister of Niki De Saint Phalle's gargantuan walk-through sculpture, *She*, whose vast interior was entered, like the biomorphic mothership in *Alien*, through a vaginal slit. At one point, Sterling's protagonist detects a strange scent: "Lindsay placed it suddenly: sex pheromones. The architecture was aroused."[41]

Perhaps the transformation of the body's penetralia, via CAT scans, endoscopy, and magnetic resonance imaging, into a final frontier for a society, says J. G. Ballard, "looking back on the Space Age," is a prelude to Sterling's erogenous architecture. Likewise, the theme parking of visceral landscapes in the "Body Wars" ride at Walt Disney World's Epcot Center—a simulated trip through the body, in pursuit of a splinter—may be an early, surreptitious beta-test for everyday existence in buildings that breathe and give off blood heat: soft machines for living that will return us, in a delicious irony, to the body even as we depart the flesh, for cyberspace.

1 Earlier, significantly different versions of this essay appeared in the "Mech In Tecture: Reconsidering the Mechanical in the Electronic Era" issue of *ANY* (*Architecture New York*) and in *21.C* (#1, 1996).

2 *Panic Encyclopedia: The Definitive Guide to the Postmodern Scene*, ed. Arthur Kroker, Marilouise Kroker, David Cook (New York: St. Martin's, 1989), 15.

3 Robert B. Reich, "On the Slag Heap of History," *The New York Times Book Review*, November 8, 1992, 15.

4 Bernard Weinraub, "Directors Battle Over GATT's Final Cut and Print," *The New York Times*, International section, 24.

5 Michael J. Mandel and others, "The Entertainment Economy," *Business Week*, March 14, 1994, 59.

6 Eric S. Raymond, *The New Hacker's Dictionary*, second edition (Cambridge, MA: MIT Press, 1993), 432.

7 Stuart Ewen, "Pragmatism's Postmodern Poltergeist," *New Perspectives Quarterly*, Volume 9, #2, (Spring, 1992): 47.

8 William Gibson, *Neuromancer* (New York: Ace, 1984), 51.

9 Mark C. Taylor, "De-Signing the Simcit," *Any*, no. 3, November/December, 1993, 11.

10 Bernard Tschumi, "Ten Points, Ten Examples," *Any*, ibid., 41.

11 Quoted in *Batman: Official Movie Souvenir Magazine* (Brooklyn: The Topps Company, 1989), 18.

12 Marshall McLuhan and Quentin Fiore, *The Medium is the Massage* (New York: Bantam, 1967), unnumbered page.

13 Eric Norden, "Playboy Interview: Marshall McLuhan," *Playboy*, March, 1969, 56.

14 Loc. cit.

15 Gary Chapman, "Taming the Computer," *Flame Wars: The Discourse of Cyberculture*, a special issue of the *South Atlantic Quarterly* (Durham, NC: Duke University Press, Fall 1993), 830-31.

16 Barbara Presley Noble, "At Work; Labor-Management Rorshach Test," *The New York Times,* June 5, 1994, 21.

17 Michael Kelley, "Urban Gothic," *Spectacle,* April 19, 1985, 6.

18 Mark Dery, "Future Noir," interview with Mike Davis, *21.C,* #3, 1995.

19 This section owes its title to the German "hardbeat" techno group of the same name, whose music is every bit as bruisingly technophallic as it sounds.

20 Claudia Springer, "Muscular Circuitry: The Invincible Armored Cyborg in Cinema," *Genders,* No. 18 (Winter 1993): 91.

21 Ibid., 89.

2 Ibid., 92.

23 Thomas Hine, *Facing Tomorrow: What the Future Has Been, What the Future Can Be* (New York: Knopf, 1991), 174.

24 Kevin Kelly, *Out of Control: The Rise of Neo-Biological Civilization* (Reading, MA: Addison-Wesley, 1994), 1.

25 Ibid., 471.

26 I explore this theme at length in my essay "Wild Nature," which appears in the 1996 Ars Electronica anthology, *Memesis.*

27 Charles Jencks, "High-Tech Slides to Organi-Tech" (excerpt from The Architecture of the Jumping Universe), *ANY: Mech in Tecture—-Reconsidering the Mechanical in the Electronic Era,* no. 10, 1995, 44.

28 Ibid., 49.

29 Ibid., 48.

30 Terence McKenna, *The Archaic Revival* (San Francisco: Harper Collins, 1991), 224.

31 Rudolf Doernach, "Biotecture," *Whole Earth Review,* Number 64, Fall 1989, inside front cover.

32 Kelly, ibid., 167.

33 William Gibson, *Idoru* (New York: G. P. Putnam's Sons, 1996), 46, 81, 83.

34 Yoshihito Osada and Simon B. Ross-Murphy, "Intelligent Gels," *Scientific American,* May 1993, 82.

35 Engineers are already building a conceptual bridge, in the form of experimental "smart" materials, that may one day meet Osada's "chemomechanical" systems halfway. Designed to actively resist earthquakes, these materials become viscous when electrified by a current transmitted by a quake's vibrations; when the tremors subside, they solidify. See Amal Kumar Naj, "Southern California Earthquake: Engineers Want New Buildings to Behave Like Human Beings," *The Wall Street Journal,* January 20, 1994, Section B, 1.

36 Marshall McLuhan, *Understanding Media: The Extensions of Man,* first edition (Cambridge, MA: MIT Press, 1994), 123.

37 Quoted in Ewen, ibid., 130.

38 Bruce Sterling, *Schismatrix* (New York: Arbor House, 1985), 251.

39 Ibid., 186.

40 Ibid., 249.

41 Ibid.

Mark Dery is a cultural critic and author of Escape Velocity: Cyberculture at the End of the Century *and* The Pyrotechnic Insanitarium: Madness and Mayhem in Millennial America. *He edited* Flame Wars: The Discourse of Cyberculture.

I SEE...

ECO-TEC INTL. CORPS

DIA 425 199314 00

I See ...
the insurgent
mechanics of infection

Mel Chin

DEFINITION

Transcript and performance notes for ECO-TEC New York
Conference. Performed at DIA Center for the Arts. April 25,
1993.

SECTION I

MISSION

1.

After introduction you have 30 seconds to . . .
Pick up Remington M700 .30-06 bolt-action sniper rifle,
altered (with wireless microphone) Raytheon Night Vision
telescopic sight, from hidden space under the panel table.
Load rifle with empty shell. Walk up to the podium and get
into position. Aim at the audience slightly above the heads
and toward the far NE corner.

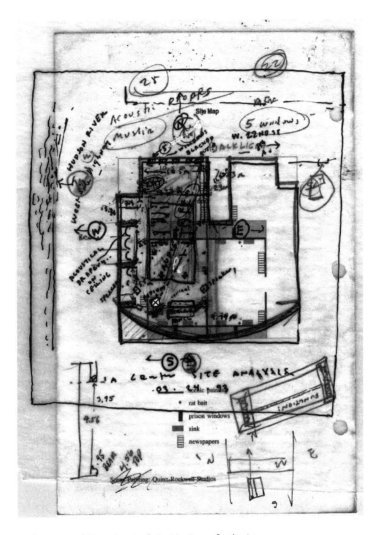

Assignment and Extraction Analysis. Dia Center for the Arts,
548 West 22nd Street, New York City. Conducted on: 03 24 93.

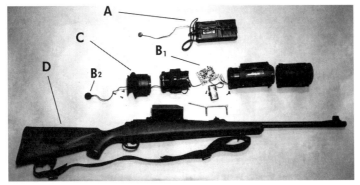

Audio Tools and Implantation Specifications. Disassembled (gutted) Raytheon Night Vision sight (Miniatured Model No. AN/PVS-3) detailing audio component insertion necessary for Mission Part 2. Note: to complete operation implant must be hardwired to existing exterior switch.

A.   *Microcassette and "wire" (input wire and earphone)*

B.₁ *Wireless transmitter (RS Cat. No. 32-1221) circuit board and 9 volt battery power source*

B.₂ *Implanted microphone*

C.   *Scope part: Rubber eyecup*

D.   *Remington M700 Rifle S/No. C6383125*

2.

Repeat these lines being input by micro tape cassette hidden in your suit . . .

> I see you and my hide is fresh.
> April—central air and non-existent wind.
> 5 northern black outs
> 2 o'clock
> 27 meter job
> 25 acoustical droops
> 43 second window
> 25 minute station
> 3 degrees
> Extraction is west
> IBS on the Hudson
> Alternate up E on eight
> Secondary heat is rising and
> Capless Assignment wears no flak.
> Conditions quiet.
> Round is ready.
> Easy.

See MISSION Requirement No.5b.
Note: speak into the eyepiece.
Voice should be amplified.

3.

Pull rifle trigger.   Audible: "click"   Sound man: "HIT"

4.

Eject the shell.

5.

a. Pull out another "gun" (small cordless Makita drill painted gun metal black) . . . undo screws that connect scope to the rifle.

b. Switch on microphone/scope and continue to follow voice on microcassette.

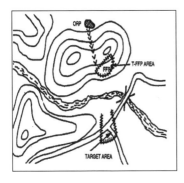

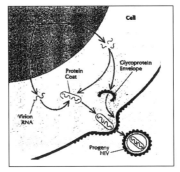

A. Hide positions.

B. HIV infection cycle.

I see you and your hide is fresh and permeable.
your passion transmission
a fluid ride
thru gates of mucosal masonry . . .
line up with platelets in the capillary crush
and flush into the arterial highway.
phagocytic cells take some

CD4 take me.

joints welded
naked . . . I am no more.
reverse transcriptase
cytoplasmic hospitality
di-ribo-nucleic ribbon gift.
doubled up into the nucleic network
incorporate, merge
and build MRNA.
protein chassis
surface parts
bond and bail out the cell
phagocytic and antibody memories return . . .

MEL CHIN

SECTION 2

6.

Put down the microphone/telescopic sight . . . read text from podium.

TEXT:

I see (. . . the insurgent mechanics of infection).

I begin with the constructed voices of two who abnormally mark the conclusion of life with unerring precision—a covert peacetime Marine sniper (whose accuracy is 98% at 1,000 meters), and a virion's pathological trek within a human host. Both are imaginefied commentary on the possession of power under specific directives—one subordinate to the Corps, who exercise the militant will of our state, the other operating under a similar code of habit, within the will of evolutionary process. The top-gun Marine prepared for duty, like the prokaryotic pared-down life form, are specialized elite entities. Both create a climate that becomes part and product of a larger, formidable psychological architecture.

I make these statements from a critical perspective of a certain body of my own work that has and continues to exercise political commentary and witness, and from a personal inability to call forth appropriate emotion and action in the light of tragedy and circumstantial reality. The purposes of the following prescriptions are reconnaissance and reflection for a method to provoke rather than invent, and to intensify the mirror rather than set conclusively in stone. This desire steadies my aim.

Artaud comments from *The Theater and Its Double*, "In the *City of God*, St. Augustine complains of this similarity between the action of the plague that kills without destroying the organs and the theater which, without killing, provokes the most mysterious alterations in the mind of not only an individual but an entire populace."

In Euripides' *Ion*, there are two drops of the Gorgon's blood that "spurted from the hollow vein"–one that cures all and one that kills all.

Microfisch document: 06 13 91.

The introduction of GP 160 (glyco protein 160 molecular weight) as a post immunological tool by Army doctors at Walter Reed Army Hospital is to be praised (the rumored mandatory inoculation of the test serum, not). My own mule-like behavior proves that things don't change that quickly. I don't expect a Gould and Eldridge punctuated equilibrium to immediately arise from the "business as usual stasis" of the military industrial complex. While this singular effort is to be applauded, will the encore be an old reactionary war tune? Will it be an aria to a future altered RNA that was as easy as taking that yellow ribbon off the old oak tree and manipulating it into a neo-fascist icon? If the antidote is first, can a more predictable and virulent one-shot-one-kill genetic poison packed in a processed gp 160 envelope be far behind? Will its delivery be through deceptive social contact? In an embrace at the next summit?

I guess I'll have to speculate and at the same time re-target my skepticism within the confines of my own discipline.

Booting artworks off high-minded pedestals is not my intention. One or two of mine are on some of the really low ones. But if I suggest that the museum and gallery systems are already acting like cult leaders gone armed and bad, could it be that I am one of the wimpy left arms of a well-intentioned institutional heartless corporate/colonial sea? All this is easy if you generate your own ink. There are works that I appreciate that have successfully penetrated the defense mechanisms and set up active critiques within established hallowed halls. But are we sucker bait? —temporary dandies, comforted and caressed by prehensile tentacles that will gradually pull us into the beak? Our protests are yummy . . . the bile we spill makes the best ink and the best release of all is the obscuring veil of a Press Release.

David Black, in his book concerning AIDS, *The Plague Years*, ends with what he describes as a cautionary tale: "The bubonic plague began in the foothills of the Himalayas in a region known as Garwhal and Kumaon. The Saracen empire acted as a buffer to protect Europe from the disease. So when the Europeans fought the Saracens during the Crusades, the more successful they were on the battlefield, the more vulnerable they were making themselves to the disease at home. Be careful what battles you win."

These scenarios represent evidence of a struggle in systems large and small; war for power between culture and state, between ethical principle and amoral prudence, and the unpredictable results between them.

Marshalling the forces necessary to wage complete warfare against existing systems as expansive as the military complex and the corporate stronghold is not a tactically secure situation. The benefits of protracted war are little. If I try to fight toe to toe— stumps will be the testament to those rounds. How can one commit to decentering power and fight what Foucault calls ". . . the

A Hide with loop holes.

I SEE ... THE INSURGENT MECHANICS OF INFECTION

fascism in us all, in our heads and everyday behavior, the fascism that causes us to love power, to desire the very thing that dominates and exploits us"?

The Hmong poet Xeng Sue Yang works another angle of the head . . .
   To cross a river I shall take off my shoes
   To cross a country I shall take off my head.

So I sit in my hide with unsettling observations, as an artist with a dissatisfaction with what I perceive to be the compartmentalization of that identity. Perhaps waging war is not what I should be doing; but the mechanics of the sniper/virus are a worthy model to use to begin the generation or survival of free thought through the infection of optional forms of reality into closed systems. An artwork that desires to take excursions into the multitude of systems that comprise our culture, other than those of gallery, museum or sanctioned public art event or space, may wish to pack a sniper/viral mind set.

Like the sniper and the virus, a fresh hide must be there for the right job and the targets should be the incubators. Specialized incubators of late modern capitalism, such as a fast food chain, a fundamentalist religious sect's compound, a tobacco corporation's advertising agency, and the less fancy endocytic pits along the ever popular strip mall, are available targets for viral action. I am reluctant to criticize these entities or even deal with them because we are mutually unhealthy within the larger body, but evolving out of this criticism is my craving for connection, and this desire for connection can propel sniper/retro-viral projects.

There are many protein cloaks available and possible to be invented in the postmodern era of art to make the connection with any unsuspecting host. There are fewer attempts to find a proper host and even less desire to remove the head or ego that is a necessary disguise to pass through this suspicious membrane.

The frightening conditions that are imposed by a sniper are no longer lurking in the historic journals of war. They are in your face though out of sight. Such mechanics need not be taken as negative models but as successful working models that are worth taking seriously. Such expeditions into these non-traditional venues are especially fat targets or assignments for art.

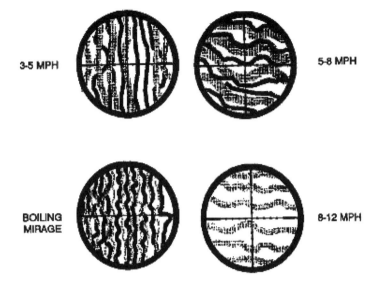

3-5 MPH

5-8 MPH

BOILING
MIRAGE

8-12 MPH

Target mirages caused by wind and heat.

Of course, should the juicy fruit get smart . . . alternate escapes must be planned. Here again is a way out through biological methodology . . . rapidly mutate and go to the next cell.

My paranoia, my vigilance, my witness, my exposure of conspiracy, is not enough. I must take more action. As eighty-something Aunt E. McRedmond, of Nashville, Tennessee, says, "Work begun is half done." It is the halfness that interests me, the middle state. So the invention of half-done, or incomplete vehicles is more essential than ever. By taking a lesson from the virion that is structurally incomplete, we have a clue. It uses a specific condition to replicate more of is own kind. I think, as an artist, I need to set up similar conditions where it is not the finality of the artst's statement that is important, but the initiation of action that is important.

There is an unpredictable aspect to all this. The attack on the Branch Davidian cult compound yielded chaotic and unforeseen effects that raised questions concerning acceptable models of human behavior. Both David Koresh and the ATF had goals final and concise. With cock-eyed optimism I can hope that mine may not be so hard-wired. I turn to the sniper and virion mechanics as a means not to undermine life, but to deploy coated,

I SEE . . . THE INSURGENT MECHANICS OF INFECTION

unadvertised, undetectable constructions to infect a condition of variables. It is an option to the bottom lines and ultimatums that breed insecurities and compel lives of conformity, fearful of and resistant to discourse, without connection to one another.

As to the nature of such a construction,
full disclosure does not exist, only the

coat has been constructed

and if I uncoat I am

no more.

Documentation: 03 25, 1993, 1400 hours (Giafranco Mantegna).

Mel Chin, sculptor, has exhibited in the United States and Europe, including the Hirshhorn Museum and Sculpture Garden, the Walker Art Center, the Menil Collection, and StoreFront for Art and Architecture. Mr. Chin produces sculptures that bear witness to political and economical tragedies. In 1995–96 he organized a public art project, In the Name of Place, *shown on prime-time television.*

Special thanks to: Anthony J. Cavella, Joel Maloney, Tamalyn Miller, Tess Miller, Helen K. Nagge, Dan Martin Rome; John Hopkins University, School of Medicine; StoreFront for Art and Architecture; DIA Center for the Arts.

Stochastic Chaos, Symmetry, and Scale Invariance

Shaun Lovejoy and D. Schertzer

Introduction: Chaos vs. Cosmos

Perhaps the oldest and most basic philosophical question is the origin of order from disorder; indeed the terms of the ancient Greek dichotomy *chaos/cosmos* are still with us. Although this problem is posed in all areas of life, it is undoubtedly in physics where it has reached its fullest and most precise expression, concomitant with the recent "chaos revolution," which has changed our outlook in so many areas. In the revolution's wake, the physics notion of *deterministic chaos* is invading territory as distant as literature and criticism.

While the validity of this attempted conceptual transplant can be criticized, the relevance of the notion to its original domain of application, physics, is rarely discussed. In this essay, we criticize the underlying philosophy of deterministic chaos as well as many of its significant claims to applications. We then show the need to develop a rather different framework which we call *stochastic chaos*. While we believe this alternative to be quite broad, potentially encompassing much of our atmospheric and geophysical environment, we do not claim exclusivity. Rather we view stochastic chaos as complementary to deterministic chaos with the former being necessary in systems involving many interacting components and the latter being useful when only a few corre-

Fig. 1 The temple at Khajuraho showing a small part of the hierarchical structure within structure architecture executed following an essentially self-similar algorithm in accord with the Hindu cosmos of smaller and smaller structures within structures.

sponding degrees of freedom are important. Both model types belong in the physicist's toolbox. While we are primarily concerned with providing a critique within physics, we have endeavored to do so in a widely accessible way.[1]

The utility of stochastic chaos lies primarily in its ability to exploit a (nonclassical) symmetry principle called "scale invariance," associated with fractals and multifractals. We will argue that the ubiquity of fractals in nature is an indication of the wide scope for applying stochastic chaos models. The basic idea of scale invariance is that small parts of a scale invariant object are similar to the whole, thus its relevance to art and architecture. For example, Trivedi argued that Indian temples from at least the tenth century onward were explicitly constructed according to fractal mathematical algorithms (fig. 1). Similarly, Briggs and Peat suggested that certain examples of Celtic art exemplify a deliberate fractal type construction.[2] The connection between art and fractals is occasionally explicit, for example, the photo album, as in "An Eye for Fractals" by McGuire.[3] More recently, a shared interest in scale invariant clouds lead us to collaborate with sculptor M. Chin on a projection piece at the StoreFront for Art and Architecture, New York City, entitled "Degrees of Paradise." This piece featured an evolving multifractal cloud simulation displayed on 16 monitors suspended from the ceiling.[4]

Order vs. Disorder and the Scientific World View

Although God(s) were traditionally invoked to explain order, their role was drastically diminished with the advent of the Newtonian revolution. By the middle of the nineteenth century, these laws had become highly abstract (thanks notably to Laplace, Hamilton, and Lagrange), while the corresponding scientific world view had become determinism. In this regard probably the most extreme views have been attributed to Laplace (1886), who went so far as to postulate a purely deterministic universe in which "if a sufficiently vast intelligence exists" it could solve the equations of motion of all the constituent particles of the Universe. In Laplace's universe, such a divine calculator could determine the past and future from the present in an abstract high dimensional "phase space."

Unfortunately, due to man's imperfect knowledge we are saddled with measurement errors that clearly involve notions of chance. This lead Laplace (following Voltaire) to identify chance and probability with ignorance. Much later, in 1870, probability was explicitly introduced into the formulation of physical laws by James Clerk Maxwell. This is the basic idea of classical Statistical Mechanics: that the unobserved or unknown degrees of freedom ("details"), are the source of "random" behavior such as fluctuations about a mean temperature. Although highly partial information is the rule, macroscopic objects are typically described by parameters such as temperature, pressure, and density. Most of the degrees of freedom, such as the positions and velocities of the constituent particles, are unimportant and can be reduced to various averages using statistics. Hence, the dichotomy of objective deterministic interactions of a large number of degrees of freedom coexisting with randomness arising from our subjective ignorance of the details.

Starting with Gibbs and Boltzman, this identification of statistics with ignorance evolved somewhat to the more objective identification of statistics with the irrelevance of most of the details;[5] however, this did not alter the deeply held prejudice that statistics were a poorman's substitute for determinism. A corollary to this was the hierarchical classification of scientific theories; fundamental theories being deterministic, the less fundamental involving randomness or ignorance.

Since then—even in spite of the Quantum revolution—this prejudice has become fairly entrenched even though a number of developments (especially in deterministic and more recently, in stochastic chaos) have occurred which make it obsolete. Unfortunately there has not been an adequate conceptual reassessment. In this essay, we outline these developments, and propose an alternative framework for chaos that we believe overcomes the limitations of strict determinism: *stochastic chaos*.

The Deterministic Chaos Revolution: The Butterfly Effect

The rigid "Newtonian" or "mechanical determinism" of Laplace runs into trouble as soon as one attempts to solve the equations of motion for anything but the most simple systems: as recognized by Poincaré, three particles are already sufficient.[6] However, the

general property of nonlinear systems of having "sensitive dependence" on initial conditions only became widely known in the
1970s. Better known as the "butterfly effect," this term denotes
the general property of nonlinear systems to amplify small perturbations—such as the possible large-scale consequences of the
flapping of a butterfly's wings on the atmospheric circulation.
Even if Laplace's calculator had both *almost* perfect information at
an initial instant (i.e. only infinitesimally small perturbations are
present) and infinite precision in its numerics, the predicted
future would not in fact be predictable. On the contrary, finite random-like "chaotic" behavior would result. With fluids, this led to
the idea that such "turbulence" arose through a short (rather than
infinite) series of instabilities, contrary to the pioneering idea of
Landau.[7] However—and this crucial point has often been over-
looked—even if only three instabilities are necessary, the asymp-
totic state of "fully developed fluid turbulence" still depends on an
infinite number of degrees of freedom!

In addition to the butterfly effect, two additional key developments were necessary to make the "chaos" revolution. The first
was the reduction of the scope of study to systems with a small
number of degrees of freedom. The second was the discovery
that under very general circumstances[8] that quantitatively the
same behavior could result—the celebrated Feigenbaum constant. This universality finally allowed for quantitative empirical
tests of the theory. By the early 1980s these developments had led
to what could properly be called the "chaos revolution."

Later Developments and Problems

The basic outlook provoked by the developments in chaos (that
random-like behavior is "normal" and not pathological) is valid
irrespective of the number of degrees of freedom of the system
in question. The success of systems with a small number of
degrees of freedom led to some bold prognostications, such as
"junk your old equations and look for guidance in clouds'
repeating patterns."[9] This fervor was unfortunately accompanied by a drastic restriction of the scope of chaos to meaning
precisely deterministic systems with few degrees of freedom.
The restriction, coupled with the development of new empirical
techniques, led to a major focus on applications and a number

of curious, if not absurd, claims.

It is perhaps easiest to understand these aberrations by considering the example of the climate system (fig. 2). Numerical modeling of the climate has always been one of the great scientific challenges, if only because of the large (practically infinite) number of degrees of freedom assumed to be involved. However, when new chaos tools were applied to the data; it was even claimed[10] that only four degrees of freedom were required to specify the state of the climate.[11] Attempts were even made to prove objectively from analysis of data that, in spite of appearances, random-like signals were in fact deterministic in origin.

These attempts were flawed at several levels, the most important of which is philosophical: the supposition that nature is (ontologically) either deterministic or random. In reality, the best that any empirical analysis could demonstrate was that specific deterministic models fit the data better (or worse) than specific stochastic ones.

The Alternative for Large Numbers of Degrees of Freedom Systems: Stochastic Chaos

We have argued that by the mid 1980s, the ancient idea of chaos had come to take on a very narrow and restrictive meaning, essentially characterizing deterministic systems with small numbers of degrees of freedom. The philosophy underlying its use as a model for complex geophysical, astrophysical, ecological, or sociological systems—each involving nonlinearly interacting spatial structures or fields—has two related aspects, each of which we argue are untenable. The first is the illogical inference that because deterministic systems can have random-like behavior, that random-like systems are best modeled as not random after all. The second is that the spatial structures which apparently involve huge variability and many degrees of freedom spanning wide ranges of scale, can in fact be effectively reduced to a small finite number. In short, at a philosophical level, deterministic chaos is an attempt to resurrect Newtonian determinism.

In order to overcome the limitations of deterministic modeling, we note that the axiomatization of probability theory early in this century clarified the objective status of probabilities and made the idea that statistics is somehow an expression of ignorance rather outdated. We follow general usage in denoting such objective randomness as "stochastic." The fundamental characteristic of stochastic theories—models which distinguishes them from their deterministic counterparts is that they are defined on probability spaces (usually infinite dimensional), whereas their deterministic counterparts are only manageable on low dimensional spaces.

The stochastic chaos alternative for nonlinear dynamics with many degrees of freedom is now easy to state: contrary to Einstein's injunction that "God does not play dice," we seek to determine "how God plays dice" with large numbers of interacting components.[12]

Objections to Stochastic Chaos

Before continuing, we should briefly consider various objections to the use of stochastic theories/models.

Fundamental theories should be deterministic : Ever since statistical mechanics forced physicists to embrace stochasticity in a major physical theory, there has been an attempt to discount the significance of this fact by claiming that at least fundamental theories should be deterministic. However, since Quantum Mechanics itself admits a completely consistent stochastic interpretation,[13] it is hard to avoid the conclusion that stochastic theories can also be fundamental.

Causality requires determinism: Another reason for clinging to determinism is the common misconception that causality is identical to determinism, or equivalently, that indeterminism implies a degree of acausality. This view has already been criticized by one of the founders of quantum mechanics, Max Born.[14] At a formal level, causality is nothing more than a specific type of objective determination or necessity, and, as emphasized by Bunge,[15] it by no means exhausts the category of physical determination that includes other kinds of lawful production/interconnection, including statistical determination.

Structures are evidence of determinism: Another common prejudice is the idea that the phenomenological identification of structures is a kind of signature of determinism, while the presence of variability without "interesting" structures is a symptom of noise. The inadequacy of this view of randomness is brought home by the (still little-known fact) that stochastic models can (in principle) explain the same phenomena; the key is a special kind of "stochastic chaos" involving a scale invariant symmetry principle in which a basic (stochastic) cascade mechanism repeats scale after scale after scale, from large to small scales, eventually building up enormous variability. The result, multifractal fields, is the subject of much of the remainder of this essay. The main point is that unlike classical noises, such stochastic processes specifically have extreme events called "singularities," which are strong enough to create structures. There is insufficient "self-averaging," the result is far from a featureless white noise.

Physical Arguments for Stochastic Chaos: The Example of Turbulence

We have already noted that since stochastic processes are defined on infinite dimensional probability spaces, stochastic models are *a priori* the simplest whenever the number of degrees of freedom is large. In particular, we argue that stochastic chaos is particularly advantageous with respect to classical approaches when a nonclassical symmetry is present: scale invariance.

Consider the example of fluid turbulence. The basic dynamical, and deterministic ("Navier-Stokes"), equations of fluid motion have been known for nearly 150 years, yet the fundamental problem remains whole: how to reconcile the (violent) nonclassical turbulent statistics/structures with the equations. If only because of this relative lack of progress, turbulence must be counted among the most difficult problems in physics. The main difficulty is the presence of a very strong type of inhomogeneity called "intermittency." Not only does the "activity" of turbulence induce inhomogeneity, but the activity itself is inhomogeneously distributed. There are "puffs" of (active) turbulence inside "puffs" of (active) turbulence.[16] It should now be no surprise that the cascade paradigm provides a convenient framework to study this phenomenology, yielding concrete models and interesting conjectures. In particular, it is now increasingly clear that a general outcome of stochastic cascades are multifractals, as shown below.

Scale Invariance Symmetries and Cascades:
Cascades and Multifractals

Scale invariant cascades have served as a paradigm of turbulence, at least since Richardson's celebrated poem in his 1922 book, *Weather Forecasting by Numerical Process*:

> Big whorls have little whorls that feed on their velocity, and little whorls
> have smaller whorls, and so on to viscosity (in the molecular sense)...

Initially this cascade was nothing more than a conceptual scheme for explaining the transfer of energy from the planetary scales (where the pole/equation temperature gradient forces the large-scale circulation), down to the small scales (roughly one millimeter) where it is dissipated by viscosity. However, a key feature of the atmospheric circulation (and more generally of turbulence) is that it is far from being homogeneous; it is intermittent in both time and space. In order to model this intermittency, many explicit multiplicative cascade models were developed. The simplest ("beta model") is obtained by making the simplistic assumption that at each cascade step, the turbulence is either dead or alive. Since the same mechanism (the "coin tossing" to decide whether the daughter eddy is kept alive or is killed) is repeated unchanged, scale after scale, the process is scale invariant; in the small scale limit the "active" regions form a geometrical fractal set of points.

Ignoring for the moment the artificiality of the straight construction lines and the factor of two break-up of eddies into subeddies, we can now take a step towards realism by introducing a slight modification: we continue to flip coins, but now we multiplicatively "boost" or "decrease" the energy flux density rather than boosting or killing the eddies (the "alpha model"). The result is a multifractal field with an infinite number of levels of activity, depending on the sequence of boosts and decreases: the sets of points exceeding a given intensity form geometric fractal sets, except that the fractal dimension (i.e. the sparseness) of each fractal set decreases as the intensity level increases.

The "alpha model" is an example of what physicists call "toy models": they are simple without being simplistic; their generic consequences are quite nontrivial. In this case, the alpha model

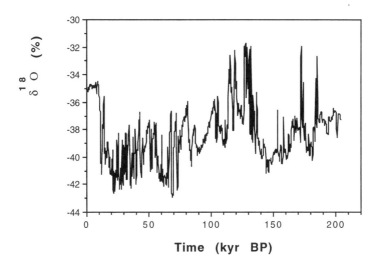

Fig. 2 High resolution (200 year average) $\delta^{18}O$ record (parts per thousand of oxygen 18 compared to to oxygen 16),coming from the recent GRIP Greenland ice core; these values are believed to be roughly proportional to the past temperature. Sharp fluctuations occuring on small time scales are clearly visible; note that the sudden warming associated with the end of the last ice age (about 10,000 years ago, far left) is by no means the only sudden transition. Schmitt et al shows that this series is scale invariant; having statistic near the theoretically predicted universal multifractal type (Schmitt et al, 1995).

Fig. 3 Multifractal cloud and mountain from the exposition "Strange Attractors: Signs of Chaos," September 14–November 26, 1989, at the Museum for Contemporary Art, New York (G. Sarma, J. Wilson).

SHAUN LOVEJOY AND D. SCHERTZER   89 has all the essential ingredients of the more sophisticated models needed for realism. Specifically, the "continuous cascade" process eliminates the discrete (factor 2) scale ratio—and hence the ugly straight-line artifacts as well as the boost/decrease dichotomy. The most important point about continuous cascades is that they generically yield "universal multifractals," special multifractals which occur irrespective of the details of the basic dynamical mechanism and depend on only three basic parameters, just like random walks discussed earlier (fig. 4).[17]

The Multifractal (Stochastic) Butterfly Effect and Self-Organized Criticality

The significance of sensitive dependence on initial conditions, the "butterfly effect," is that if the system is sufficiently unstable, then a small disturbance can grow, totally modifying the future state of the system. In the atmosphere this would mean that the sequence of weather events (which would include Texas tornadoes in Lorenz's metaphor) would be different, although presumably not the climate (which is a kind of ill-defined "average weather"). In our stochastic multifractal cascade model, we may identify an analogous "stochastic butterfly effect" by studying the small scale limit of the cascade and by determining under which conditions the small scale can dominate the large.

Contrary to "additive" stochastic chaos, such as Brownian motion, the turbulent activity around a given point is not changed by smaller and smaller amounts as cascades proceed to smaller and smaller scales; rather, it is modulated by random factors. It turns out that these lead to extreme events that are governed by nonstandard statistics characterized by algebraic (rather than exponential) probability tails, exactly the same type as those associated with avalanches and "self-organized critical phenomena."[18] However, contrary to Bak's original "sand pile model," which is a system nearly at thermodynamic equilibri-

Fig. 4 Universality of random variables illustrated by two random walks. Steps are chosen randomly to be up, down, left, or right with equal probability. On the left of each pair of columns, the steps are all of equal length, whereas on the right of each pair of columns they are occasionally five times longer (the lengths have been normalized so that the variances are the same). For a small number of steps, the walks are very different, but for a large number, they tend to the same limit and look similar.

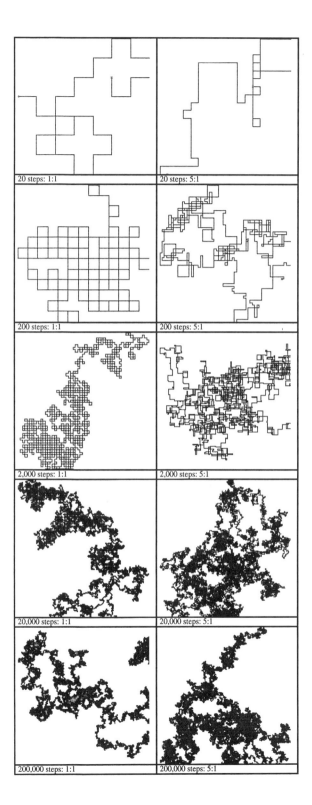

20 steps: 1:1   20 steps: 5:1

200 steps: 1:1   200 steps: 5:1

2,000 steps: 1:1   2,000 steps: 5:1

20,000 steps: 1:1   20,000 steps: 5:1

200,000 steps: 1:1   200,000 steps: 5:1

um, one has to consider a nonclassical self-organized criticality[19] in a stochastic framework. This is the multifractal/cascade version of the butterfly effect: most of the time, the flapping of the wings will lead to nothing special; the perturbation will be small compared to the existing large-scale weather structures. However, in all probability, the overall effect of the small-scale dynamics (which includes those small enough to be perturbed by a butterfly's flapping) will occasionally dominate the effect of the large-scale dynamics. This specific cascade prediction has been verified empirically in a dozen or so geophysical fields.

Nonclassical (Anisotropic) Zooms and Generalized Scale Invariance

Up to this point, we have considered scale invariance intuitively using the example of cascade processes, in which a simple mechanism is repeated scale by scale (coin tossing and multiplicative modulation). This mechanism is the same in all directions (isotropic); the resulting fractals and multifractals are therefore "self-similar" in the sense that a small piece when blown up using a standard isotropic "zoom" statistically resembles the whole. With the minor exception of "self-affinity," which involves squashing along a coordinate axis, self-similarity is the very special case discussed by Mandelbrot,[20] and in most of the fractal/multifractal literature. However, no natural system is exactly isotropic; many physical mechanisms exist that can introduce preferred directions, the most obvious being gravity. Gravity, for example, leads to a differentially stratified atmosphere: ocean and earth interior. Sources of anisotropy that can lead to differential rotation are the Coriolis force (due to the earth's rotation) or stresses (in fluids or rock) induced by external boundary conditions. Contrary to the conventional wisdom equating scale invariance with self-similarity, and hence with isotropy, scale invariance still survives, although the notion of scale undergoes a profound change. The resulting formalism of Generalized Scale Invariance (GSI) involves essentially two ingredients.[21] The first is the definition of a unit (reference) scale; the second is a family of scale-changing operators (i.e., rules) that describe how the unit scale is blown up or down. The fundamental restriction is that the rule should only involve ratios of scales so that there is no absolute notion of size (the reference scale is arbitrary). Mathematically, this implies that the scale changes form a mathematical group with a corresponding group generator. Perhaps the key factor to note is that the great differences in the appearance of the shape at different scales does not imply the existence of a characteristic scale whatsoever. Any member of the family could be taken as the unit shape and mapped onto any of the others simply by blowing up or down anisotropically by an appropriate ratio. Physically, in GSI the distribution of conserved (turbulent) fluxes determines the notion of size; this relation between scale and dynamics is analogous to that of General Relativity between the distribution of matter and energy and the metric.

The most interesting application of this is in the modeling and analysis of multifractals, for example clouds with various scale invariant generators (fig. 3). Changing the generator has the effect of changing cloud or mountain morphology/type. With GSI, we may no longer infer that such phenomenological differences in appearance necessarily correspond to differences in dynamics.

Symmetries and Dynamics

Having argued that even for a mathematically well defined deterministic problem such as hydrodynamic turbulence (the Navier-Stokes equations), the basic obstacle is an adequate treatment of the scale invariance symmetry: the "puffs within puffs." On the other hand, with practically no ingredients beyond this symmetry, stochastic cascades provide immediate insights: universal multifractals in which all the statistics are characterized by only three fundamental exponents. Just as a complete description of the dynamical equations is theoretically sufficient to specify the evolution of a system, a complete knowledge of the relevant symmetries will also suffice. This idea, applied to the turbulent cascade approach suggests that the latter would be equivalent to the usual deterministic approach if the remaining symmetries (i.e., other than scale invariance) of the fluid equations were known.

The Emergence of Stochastic Chaos from Determinism

Physics is an evolving hierarchy of interlocking theories. Statistical mechanics, at the same time, has accustomed us to the fact that methods and concepts necessary to understand large numbers of degrees of freedom (atoms/molecules in the latter) are qualititatively different from those that describe only a few. While we expect no contradiction between the theories that describe systems of a few and of many degrees of freedom (e.g., between classical mechanics and classical statistical mechanics), the idea that stochasticity is a significant "emergent quality" is not new.

In the frontier between low and high numbers of degrees of freedom, randomness emerges from determinism. Although hydrodynamic turbulence is an apparently mathematically well-defined deterministic problem, and few doubt the mathematical correctness of the equations (or their physical usefulness when only a few degrees of freedom are excited), they have been singularly unhelpful in elucidating the nature of turbulence with many degrees of freedom. A promising recent approach is a deterministic cascade model, the "Scaling Gyroscopes Cascade,"[22] which confirms with many new insights the general intuition that the chaos of turbulence is related to an infinite dimensional space (the infinite number of tops in SGC); it is also related to the complex interplay between determinism and randomness rather their simple opposition.

The Consequences: How Bright, How Hot, How Windy, is the Coast of Brittany?

We have argued that nonlinear scale invariant dynamics generically leads to a special type of stochastic chaos (universal multifractals) and that the existence of fractal structures is evidence for such multifractality. The basic feature of such scale invariant systems is that all their usual properties depend on the scale at which they are measured or observed, the exceptions being precisely the exponents such as the fractal dimensions which are scale invariant. Probably the first explicit recognition of the resolution dependence problem was by Perrin on the question of the tangent of the coast of Brittany;[23] the mathematically equivalent problem of the length was addressed in the 1950s by

Steinhaus for the left bank of the river Vistula.

Richardson quantified this effect empirically by measuring the scaling exponents of the coast of Britain and of several frontiers using the "Richardson dividers" method.[24] Shortly afterwards, in the 1967 celebrated paper, "How Long is the Coast of Britain?," Mandelbrot interpreted Richardson's scaling exponent in terms of fractal dimensions.[25] By the 1980s, it had become generally accepted that the length of a coastline was primarily a function of the resolution of the map.

Turning to the example of the atmosphere, the relevant multifractal question is "how hot, how windy, how wet, how bright is the coast of Brittany?"[26] There is now growing evidence (especially of the multifractal nature of cloud brightness fields as measured by satellite) supporting widespread multifractality. Hence, the answer depends on the space-time resolution at which the temperature, wind speed, and rain rate is measured.

Limits to Predictability and Stochastic Forecasting

There are major differences between the way in which deterministic and stochastic systems are forecast. We have already outlined the usual approach for forecasting global weather, which involves solving the highly nonlinear governing equations starting from very limited initial data, an approach limited by the computer's inability to model structures smaller than several hundred kilometers. The scale invariance symmetry is broken: over the remaining factor of 100 million or so the atmosphere is assumed homogeneous. In contrast, stochastic forecasts respect the scale invariance symmetry and (statistically) take into account interactions over the entire range of about ten billion in scale.

Considering next the nature of the stochastic forecast, we find that it is conceptually quite different from its deterministic counterpart. The deterministic forecast attempts to predict the smallest detail far ahead in the future. In contrast, a stochastic forecast could be directly related to the probability of an event occurring, as well as the statistical reliability of that probability. While conventional deterministic forecasts have been the object of 40 years or more of scientific development, the corresponding stochastic forecasts are still in their infancy. They are nevertheless promising.[27]

Conclusions

The idea of chaos can be traced back to antiquity, in art, at least to Da Vinci. Ever since Newton provided the prototypical model of deterministic, regular, nonchaotic motion for the solar system, chaos has been a recurring theme in physics. Laplace and others elevated this Newtonian determinism to a pedestal: all physical law should aspire to its form, randomness and chance being disdainfully ascribed to ignorance (Voltaire's "chance is nothing"). However, as physical theory evolved to encompass more phenomena, physics was led to the introduction of physical laws featuring intrinsic randomness, starting with Maxwell's distribution of molecular velocities. Initially, this randomness was regarded as an expression of ignorance; in the twentieth century, however, probability theory was axiomatized to make clear that randomness can be objective, or "stochastic." While it seems only natural to model chaotic, randomlike behavior with stochastic models, this obvious step has faced resistance due to strong residual prejudices in favor of the Newtonian world view. With the discovery in the 1960s that even simple nonlinear deterministic systems with as few as three degrees of freedom (interacting components) could have randomlike chaotic behavior, unreconstructed Newtonian determinism experienced a revival: such "deterministic chaos" promised to provide a deterministic explanation of randomness, finally placing it within the Newtonian orbit. The study of nonregular, nonsmooth behavior became suddenly respectable; chaotic behavior was discerned in field after field and by the end of the 1970s it was rapidly becoming the norm. This fundamental change in world view is the enduring kernel of the "chaos revolution."

An unfortunate effect of the revolution was the restriction of the notion of chaos to systems with deterministic evolution laws; further developments led to a further important limitation. Initially, nonlinear systems with few degrees of freedom were studied as simplified caricatures of systems with many degree of freedom, especially fluid turbulence. However, following the explosion of developments in these simple systems, deterministic chaos became correspondingly restricted. By the 1980s the caricature was often mistaken for the reality, leading to a number of unfortunate attempts to explain many complex random-like systems (including the weather and climate) with only a handful of degrees of freedom.

In this essay we have argued that when many interacting components are present, as is typically the case in turbulent or turbulent-like systems involving nonlinearly interacting spatial structures/fields, a more appropriate paradigm is "stochastic chaos," objective random models involving probability spaces and an infinite number of degrees of freedom. Indeed, following the example of statistical mechanics, stochastic approaches are natural to use in high dimensional systems. Stochasticity is then a quality "emergent" from low dimensional deterministic theories as the latter are extrapolated to many degrees of freedom.

To date, the primary utility of stochastic chaos is the facility with which it enables us to exploit a nonclassical symmetry: scale invariance. Scale invariance is much richer than is usually supposed, providing for example, a potentially unifying paradigm for geophysics (and possibly astrophysics). Probably the most familiar examples of scale invariant objects are geometric fractal sets; however, fields such as the temperature, wind, and cloud brightness/density are much more interesting. These are multifractals, which are generically produced in cascade processes. Such cascades involve a dynamical generator which repeats scale after scale from large to small structures (in the atmosphere, eddies). In this way, it builds up tremendous (nonclassical) variability, which need not be self-similar (isotropic, the same in all directions). Such anisotropic scale invariance requires the formalism of Generalized Scale Invariance (GSI) to define new (anisotropic) ways of "zooming"/"blowing up" structures. In GSI the system's dynamics determines the very notion of size. Although this has not yet occurred explicitly, we may expect that these new notions of size and scale will find both scientific and artistic expression.

Twenty years ago, the dominant scientific view was that most interesting physical systems were "smooth," "regular," and predictable. The *deterministic chaos* revolution has made such a view seem strangely antiquated; chaotic, unpredictable variability is now the norm. In spite of this undeniable change in viewpoint, there have been few decisive applications. We believe that this is because most interesting systems have many degrees of freedom; therefore, stochastic chaos combined with the scale invariance symmetry ("multifractals") may allow the chaos revolution to take a step forward by bringing large numbers of degrees of freedom systems into its purview.

1 This paper is an abridged version of a much longer paper available from the authors.

2 J.Briggs and Peat, *Turbulent Mirror: An Illustrated Guide to Chaos Theory and the Science of Wholeness* (Touchstone Books: New York, 1989).

3 M. McGuire, *An Eye for Fractals: A Graphic and Photographic Essay* (Addison-Wesley: Redwood City, CA, 1991).

4 This collaboration eventually led to participation in the ECO-TEC II International forum (1993) and to the presentation of an earlier version of this paper.

5 See A. Dahan Dalmedico, "Le determinisme de Pierre-Simon Laplace et le determinisme aujourd'hui," in *Chaos et determinisme*, edited by J.L.C. A. Dahan Dalmedico, K. Chemla (Editions du Seuil: Paris, 1992), 371–406.

6 H. Poincaré, *Les Méthodes Nouvelles de la Méchanique Céleste* vol. I (Gautier-Villars: Paris, 1892).

7 L. Landau, *C. R. (Dokl.) Academy of Science USSR* 44 (1944): 311.

8 M. J. Feigenbaum, "Quantitative Universality for a Class of Nonlinear Transformations," *Journal of Statistical Physics* 19 (1978): 25; S. Grossman and S. Thomae, "Invariant Distributions and Stationary Correlation Functions of One-Dimensional Discrete Processes," *Zeitschrift für Naturforschung a* 32 (1977): 1353–363.

9 P. Cvitanovic, *Universality in Chaos* (Philadelphia: Adam Hilger, 1984).

10 C. Nicolis and G. Nicolis, "Is There a Climate Attractor?," *Nature* 311 (1984): 529.

11 See P. Grassberger,"Do Climate Attractors Exist?," *Nature* 323 (1986): 609, for an early technical criticism.

12 D. Schertzer and S. Lovejoy, "Nonlinear Variability in Geophysics: Multifractal Analysis and Simulation," in *Fractals: Physical Origin and Consequences*, edited by L. Pietronero (Plenum: New York, 1989), 49.

13 E. Nelson, *Physics Review* 150 (1966): 1079; D. Bohm and B.J. Hiley, *The Undivided Universe: An Ontological Interpretation of Quantum Theory* (Routledge: London, 1993); M. Bunge, "Causality, Chance and Law," *American Scientist* 49 (1961): 432–48; M. Bunge, *Foundations of Physics* (Springer: New York, 1967).

14 Max Born, *Atomic Physics*, 1956; 8th revised edition (New York: Dover, 1989).

15 M. Bunge "Causality, Chance and Law," 432–48.

16 G.K. Batchelor and A.A. Townsend, "The Nature of Turbulent Motion at Large Wavenumbers," *Proceedings of the Royal Society of London* A199 (1949): 238.

17 D. Schertzer and S. Lovejoy, "Physical modeling and Analysis of Rain and Clouds by Anisotropic Scaling of Multiplicative Processes," *Journal of Geophysical Research* 92 (1987): 9693–714.

18 P. Bak, C. Tang, and K. Weiessenfeld, "Self-Organized Criticality: An Explanation of 1/f Noise," *Physical Review Letter* 59 (1987): 381–84.

19 D. Schertzer and S. Lovejoy, "The Multifractal Phase Transition Route to Self-Organized Criticality in Turbulence and Other Dissipative Nonlinear Systems," *Physics Reports* (1998).

20 B.B. Mandelbrot, "How Long is the Coastline of Britain? Statistical Self-Similarity and Fractional Dimension," *Science* 155 (1967): 636–38; Mandelbrot,

The Fractal Geometry of Nature (Freeman: San Francisco, 1983).

21 S. Lovejoy and D. Schertzer, "Scale Invariance, Symmetries, Fractals and stochastic Simulations of Atmospheric Phenomena," *Bulletin of the American Medical Society* 67 (1986): 21–32; S.S. Pecknold, S. Lovejoy, D. Schertzer, and C. Hooge, "Multifractals and the Resolution Dependence of Remotely Sensed Data: Generalized Scale Invariance and Geographical Information Systems," in *Scaling in Remote Sensing and Geographical Information Systems*, edited by M.G.D. Quattrochi (Lewis: Boca Raton, FL, 1997), 361–94.

22 Y. Chigirinskaya and D. Schertzer, "Cascade of Scaling Gyroscopes: Lie Structure, Universal Multifractals and Self-Organized Criticality in Turbulence," in *Stochastic Models in Geosystems*, edited by W. Woyczynski and S. Molchansov, (Springer-Verlag: New York, 1996), 57–82; Chigirinskaya, D. Schertzer, and S. Lovejoy, "Scaling Gyroscopes Cascade: Universal Multifractal Features of 2D and 3D Turbulence," *Fractals and Chaos in Chemical Engineering*, CFIC 96 (Rome, 1996), 371–84.

23 J. Perrin, *Les Atomes* (NRF-Gallimard: Paris, 1913).

24 L.F. Richardson, "The Problem of Contiguity: An Appendix of Statistics of Deadly Quarrels," *General Systems Yearbook* 6 (1961): 139–87.

25 B.B. Mandelbrot, "How Long is the Coastline of Britain? Statistical Self-Similarity and Fractional Dimension," *Science* 155 (1967): 636–38.

26 S. Lovejoy and D. Schertzer, "How Bright is the Coast of Brittany?," in *Fractals in Geoscience and Remote Sensing*, edited by G. Wilkinson (Office for Official Publications of the European Communities: Luxembourg, 1995), 102–51.

27 D. Marsan, D. Schertzer, and S. Lovejoy, "Causal Space-Time Multifractal Processes: Predictability and Forecasting of Rain Fields," *Journal of Geophysical Research* 31D no. 26 (1996): 333–26, 346; F. Schmitt, S. Lovejoy, and D. Schertzer, "Multifractal Analysis of the Greenland Ice-core Project Climate Data," *Geophysical Research Letter* 22 (1995): 1689–92; S.S. Pecknold, S. Lovejoy, D. Schertzer, and C. Hooge, "Multifractals and the Resolution Dependence of Remotely Sensed Data: Generalized Scale Invariance and Geographical Information Systems," in *Scaling in Remote Sensing and Geographical Information Systems* (1997), 361–94.

Shaun Lovejoy has served as Professor Of Physics, McGill University, in Montreal, Canada, since 1985. His work centers on scale variance, fractals in turbulent and chaotic systems, and their geophysical applications to weather and climate. He is coeditor of Nonlinear Variability in Geophysics: Scaling and Fractals.

D. Schertzer is director of the Laboratory in Mechanical Modeling, University P.& M. Curie, in Paris, France

SHAUN LOVEJOY AND D. SCHERTZER

Topology of an Island City

Jean Gardner

Mention New York City and most people picture the Statue of Liberty, Times Square, or the Empire State Building. Few imagine, or actually see, the magnificent natural environment of the city and its variety of animal life.[1] The idea of New York City as part of the Earth community may come as a surprise.[2] Most people know that we have built New York as well as many other cities in ways that disrupt natural systems. This disruption, however, does not mean that cities are separate from the functioning of the Earth. Beavers dam streams that change the surrounding ecology. We consider beaver dams part of nature. Why should we think of cities as separate from nature?

Where is the Earth in New York City?

It is in the city's waterbodies: the bays, the Hudson, East, and Harlem Rivers, and the Atlantic Ocean. It is in the city's numerous islands: Manhattan, Staten, Ellis, City, Riker's, Hart, Roosevelt, Governor's, Shooter's, Prall's, North, and South Brother; and in the countless marshes in Jamaica Bay and in Brooklyn and Queens on Long Island. It is also in the city's mainland peninsula known as The Bronx.

The Earth is visible also in the city's parks. Despite a population of over seven million, more than one-fourth of New York's acreage, nearly 50,000 acres, remains parkland owned

Dead Horse Bay, Gateway National Recreation Area, New York (Joel Greenberg).

by the city, state, and the federal government. Adjacent to Kennedy Airport lies a 9,000-acre salt marsh with swaying feathery grasses. Nearby devastated neighborhoods in The Bronx grows a centuries-old forest with a hemlock grove. Chemical refineries in southwest Staten Island stand close to a 75-million-year-old sandy environment of scrub trees and shrubs that, in the past, following fires caused by lightning or human carelessness, would regenerate periodically. Now the New City Department of Parks prevents this process from occurring, creating a tinderbox.

New York's native natural environment, quite unexpectedly, is the most varied found in any American city. Within the city limits exist visible bedrock, valleys, hills, ridges, bluffs, beaches, woods, and meadows. These varied lands are complemented by an extensive water system. From the highest point on Manhattan in Fort Tryon Park, we can see the Hudson River, which is the southern-most fjord in the world. The existence of the fjord means that a glacier, the Wisconsin Glacier, sculpted the riverbed for this waterbody some 15,000 years ago. What we witness from this high place along the Hudson River is the impact of a force of nature that many believe can surpass forces unleashed by human activities.

Earth systems also function in architecture, just as they do in urban parks and vacant lots. Yet the way we build our cities with roads and large buildings prevents us from being aware of the natural dynamics in which cities are embedded—a dynamic which ultimately limits our cities and ourselves.[3] For instance, consider Manhattan in the larger context of time. The contemporary period is currently in the midst of the island's second mountain building era. Geological forces created the island's first mountains eons ago, but human forces are presently shaping the second range of high peaks. As we build these "mountains" of buildings, or what most call architecture, we alter air currents on Manhattan Island, change the way the sun falls in the city, and also redirect the flow of water and energy. Simultaneously, we encourage more and more people to visit and live here. As a result, we need to produce artificial heat and light, to cool air, and to import water and food to survive— changes that now mediate all our activities.

Natural events occurring within these humanly-manipulated systems have become crises in some instances. Periodic dips in the levels of spring snowmelts and rain result in having to conserve water during the summer months. A heat wave in July and August combined with trapped ozone from automobiles, forces the elderly and children to stay inside. A snow blizzard in winter scrambles traffic and costs merchants millions of dollars in lost business.

Our ongoing building activity intensifies, manipulates, and transforms the local ecology but does not ultimately free us from its constraints. When we talk about redesigning Manhattan as a more ecologically sound habitat, we must remember that no island functions in isolation from the Earth's systems. On the Earth, architecture and ecology function as one extremely complex, interrelated system.[4]

For example, New York City's tallest buildings are deliberately concentrated in the Wall Street and Midtown Manhattan areas. This is where the bedrock of the island is near the surface, thus providing a natural and solid foundation upon which to construct such high buildings. In contrast, the location of Canal Street follows the edge of what were once marshy inlets that separated Manhattan into two islands at high tide. Consequently the buildings along Canal Street are low; high buildings would need artificial floating foundations, similar to those found in Chicago, making them more expensive and complex to construct.

New York City straddles the southernmost edge of the Wisconsin Glacier, which created the Hudson River bed. The southernmost edge of this mile-high ice sheet, known as a moraine, can be visualized by imagining a diagonal line drawn across Long Island from the North Shore to the Verrazano-Narrows Bridge, and then across Staten Island to New Jersey by way of the Outerbridge crossing over Arthur Kill. North of the glacier, along the rocky coasts of New England, the land bears the marks of the ice; south of it along the mid-Atlantic beaches is land formed by the outwash from the melting ice. The demarcation of the moraine, in turn, affects where certain plants and animals live. New York City exists as a single bioregion that represents a crossroads and a hub for a diverse northern and southern life zones. Could there be a relationship between this bio-regional diversity and the diversity of the city's human popula-tion and its architecture?

A bioregion is the ecological area formed by a watershed draining into a river, a bay or an ocean. The way to understand the ecological functioning of Manhattan, including its buildings, roads, and other human activities, is to think bioregionally. Every bioregion has a particular geology, biology, and zoology, even though its boundaries are dynamic and in constant flux. The animals, including humans, living in each bioregion adapt their lives to their respective bioregion, thus developing distinc-tive cultures. Every bioregion, in turn, impacts neighboring bioregions. New York City is part of the Hudson River Valley Bioregion.[5] The ecological impact of New York City, however, reaches to James Bay in Canada and its Hydro-Quebec project, which includes plans to flood the ancestral lands of the Cree people to supply electricity to New Yorkers. It reaches to the myriad sources of food to feed the city.

At the largest scale, the Hudson River Bioregion impacts the entire planet. James Lovelock, a British atmospheric chemist, has argued that the Earth is a self-regulating entity, which he calls Gaia. He has convinced many that the planet is one, uni-fied, and complex system of communication and control that adjusts the temperature of the surface of the Earth and the chemical composition of the atmosphere to make life possible. Lovelock's studies indicate that life on Earth is highly improba-ble; as the temperature of the sun increases, the Earth's tem-perature should rise and life on earth should be increasingly dif-ficult to sustain. Instead, the planet adjusts its temperature to sustain life on Earth's surface. Yet as humans continue to cover the Earth with architecture and other constructions, such as we see in New York City, we disrupt these adjustments and change the features of the earth's surface that help keep its tempera-tures suitable for life as we know it.[6]

Architecture functions as part of Gaia, regardless of whether it contributes beneficially to the planet's health. For most of the time that homosapiens have roamed the Earth, peo-ple sheltered themselves with materials that were available to them nearby. Building with local materials makes it more probable that we will create feedback loops between buildings and Gaia to sustain local ecological systems. Local materials have evolved over centuries in relation to the materials' and a particular region's ecology, adapting to these ecologies. In addition, minimal energy is expanded in transporting the materials from the place of origin to the site where they will be used. Consequently, for centuries the building activities of homosapiens did not dramatically disturb Gaia, whose processes today are being changed by human constructions.

Freshkills landfill in Staten Island attests to the building habits of the last hundred years, which are changing Gaia. One of the highest points near the Atlantic Ocean, this dump site contains non-renewable and renewable building materials from far-flung parts of the Earth. Much energy was expended in getting these materials to New York City and then using them. Many of these materials could be reused and/or recycled. Instead, they are considered waste.

The local ecologies of cities result from centuries of mutual adaptation between vegetation, wildlife populations, a geographical location, and the urban settlement. One example is salt marshes located within or near a city. Salt marshes nurture many of the plants and fishes that make coastlines rich food suppliers for humans; they are also the most powerful filters and pollution detoxifiers on the planet. The relatively self-regulating feedback systems of salt marshes also regulate local and global temperatures. Marshes modulate surrounding climates, helping, in many cases, to make a particularly suitable place for human life to thrive along a seaboard.

Such marshes once constituted thousands of acres of New York City's coastlines; once, over 3,000 acres of wetlands edged The Bronx section of the city alone. Now there are less than 50 acres remaining in The Bronx. The Pelham Bay Landfill was built in one of these marshes, contaminating surrounding Long Island Sound. The Gaia Institute of the Cathedral of St. John the Divine has developed a strategy to deal with the Pelham Bay Landfill using bioremediation and ecological restoration to surround the landfill with several acres of salt marsh that are capable of processing many times the pollutants discharged from the landfill, thus reversing years of degradation.

Similarly, the Institute has persuaded the Department of Environmental Protection in New York City to allow it to reconstitute highly polluted Oakland Ravine as part of a city treatment project of the area's stormwater runoff. Near the border of Queens borough, close to the tidal marshes of Alley Pond Park, the Institute is planting native species, stabilizing hill slopes, and restoring wetlands so that storm runoff will be cleaned before entering the city's estuaries. Without these changes, storm runoff dumps a staggering load of nitrates, suspended solids, and hydrocarbons into these life-supporting waterbodies without benefiting the local aquifer. The cost will be one-tenth of what the city would have spent building storm sewers.[7]

We are now increasingly aware that humanity's survival is inextricably linked to the survival of the Earth. Present ecological systems have become extremely vulnerable through humans' efforts to survive without them, or inspite of them. These recent New York City projects represent constructive efforts to achieve local sustainability, and to enter into a reciprocal relation with the Earth. This mutually beneficial relation can help engender much more than the health of earth, air, energy, water, and animal species within our cities. It can aid in creating a sense a well-being for the people who live in them, a sense of dwelling in place that creates the feeling that this is where one belongs, that this is home.

1 Jean Gardner, *Urban Wilderness: Nature in New York City* (New York: Earth Environmental Group, 1988).

2 Thomas Berry, " The Hudson River Valley: A Bioregional Story," *The Dream of the Earth* (San Francisco: Sierra Club Books, 1988).

3 Gregory Bateson, "Form, Substance, and Difference" and "Ecology and Flexibility in Urban Civilization," *Steps to an Ecology of Mind* (Northvale, NJ: James Aronson, 1972)

4 Nancy Jack Todd and John Todd, *From Eco-Cities to Living Machines: Principles of Ecological Design* (Berkeley: North Atlantic Books, 1994).

5 Doug Aberley, ed., *Boundaries of Home: Mapping for Local Empowerment.* (Philadelphia: New Society Publishers, 1993).

6 J.E. Lovelock, Gaia: *A New Look at Life on Earth.* (New York and London: Oxford University Press, 1979).

7 Jean Gardner, "Sustainable Cities," A Paper Prepared for the Second United Nations Conference on Human Settlements, *Habitat II* (June 3-14, 1996), Istanbul (New York: Cathedral of St. John the Divine, 1996).

Richmond Brook, Egbertville Ravine, The Greenbelt (Joel Greenberg).

Jean Gardner is the author of Urban Wilderness: Nature in New York City, *and professor of History and Theory, Department of Architecture and Environmental Design, Parsons School of Design. Her research is concerned with making the built environment an optimal part of the Earth Community.*

Jewel in the Balance

James Wines

As the world enters the new era of the Age of Information and Ecology, ECO-TEC offers a forum on relevant issues facing the next decade. It was in this same spirit over sixty years ago that another theoretical discourse defined the principles of Modern design, beginning with an eventful symposium known as the Athens Charter. The Charter's organizers intended to shape the future of the building arts in response to an emerging Age of Industry and Technology. To consolidate the dialogue, a group of leading architects and designers, including Le Corbusier, organized a yacht trip through the same Mediterranean waters we look out on from the island of Corsica.

The mission statement that emerged from the Athens Charter voyage clearly connected art and architecture with engineering and science. Advocates of this new esthetic also believed in a direct equation between art and a socialist vision for habitat, and that this criteria would reshape people's lives. They were right to an extent. The only problem, in retrospect, was that the spoils of the Industrial Revolution and its effects on architecture, notably the proliferation of ugly and wasteful buildings constructed in the name of Modernism, have visually and environmentally destroyed large parts of the world.

The obsession with technology has been devastating to what

Corte citadel, Corsica (Mel Chin).

we now seek as "quality of life." The more environmentally sensitive urban and suburban dwellers today agonize over the question of how, for example, America became a nation saturated with ubiquitous shopping malls, multilane roads, and faceless megastructures. Today, Western civilization seems to have arrived at an important threshold, where the Industrial Revolution and its manifestations in Modernism and Constructivism have become synonymous with environmental destruction, or what Heidegger has referred to as "debased techne." The well-founded idealism of building and progress that launched this century has in the last decade become conceptually and intellectually identified with the opposite culture that responsible artists and architects abide by in the ecologically-oriented 1990s. We have passed from an industrial and technologically driven past to a future where a concern for the earth and its significance for the survival of all life dominates public consciousness and the imagery of the arts. Generating and distributing information and creating the tools for environmental protection depend on technology, but there is no reason why this revolution must be psychologically, politically, or economically bound to the destructive legacy of heavy industry and its dependence on the waste of fossil fuels.

One question that arose during discussions in Corsica was why foreigners, who themselves arrive from the very profligate industrial societies we bemoan, have invaded this pastoral island with their dialogue. One can certainly understand Corsican residents asking, "What can these people offer us?" The question should be reversed. Instead, visitors should ask, "what can this island teach us?" An important lesson stems from the quality of life in Corsica and the historical fusion of architecture with nature. At the same time, with ample evidence of rapidly encroaching environmental destruction in Corsica, the residents may also have something to learn from the mistakes of societies represented by foreign participants.

Returning to the Athens Charter analogy, it is interesting to realize that both Le Corbusier and Jose Luis Sert were also inspired by the Mediterranean context, and retained this influence throughout their professional lives, in spite of their advocacy of the Machine Age as a source of imagery. Now, it would seem, we have come full circle. Reviving the spirit of the Athens

Charter discourse presents an opportunity to refine the original mission by placing technology in the background and advancing the "Mediterranean idea" as the foundation for a new environmental art and architecture. In this regard, the ECO-TEC project should emphasize the "Eco" more than the "Tec."

Our insurgent Age of Information and Ecology calls for different premises than the Age of Industry and Technology, new tenets that grasp where the building arts stand relative to the environmental initiative. In architecture, this earlier legacy has left us with some sobering statistics. The construction of human shelter consumes one-sixth of the world's fresh water supply, one-quarter of its wood harvest, and two-fifths of its fossil fuels and manufactured materials. As a result, builders of the next millennium must embrace a radically changed philosophy for preservation and new construction to reverse the continuing trend toward omnivorous construction technologies and thoughtless waste. In its place, any relevant and responsible architecture must be conceived in harmony with nature.

Many people view ecology as largely the responsibility of others, apart from systematic recycling of garbage that has become a part of most daily lives. Among urban dwellers, nature is perceived as a highly complex force that most deem important, but not important enough to override such technocentric and anthropocentic concerns as a booming economy, job security, and government entitlements. The natural environment, in simplified terms, is seen as a place where they drive to on weekends. Because the subject is so vast and the apocalyptic consequences so terrifying, there is a tendency for the general populace to shut the subject out of mind, and for governments to find the long-term protection of nature more threatening than the short-term security of political expedience. If this resistance to reality does not change globally, there will be no politics to worry about. The human species will simply become extinct. The radical, "deep ecologists" suggest this would be no great loss, believing that homosapiens are an ecological aberration, a global cancer to be eradicated, and the earth should be returned to the earthworm. As an artist and architect, however, I remain optimistic about the capacity of human intelligence to resolve problems and the strength of survival instinct to sustain our species.

JAMES WINES

Certainly no art form will save the earth. The arts can monitor society and its behavior, deliver strong social and political messages, influence popular views, and become metaphorical messengers for some philosophical direction or consensus ideology. Indeed, the earlier architectural movements of this century were more ambitious in their motivation to change the world. Le Corbusier articulated the choice of the New Age as a condition of "architecture or revolution," in that society would either adapt to his new order or perish from proletariat rebellion and bourgeoisie stagnation. Only the most egocentric architects would believe this today.

The Garden as Metaphor

The garden may be viewed as a threshold of entry into many ideas and issues of our time. This does not mean interpreting ecology and the inclusion of landscape as isolated green sanctuary amidst hostile surroundings. Rather, the garden today can be a source of urbanistic fulfillment, as well as a rich and influential reservoir of imagery for artists and architects. At the end of *Candide*, Voltaire's saga of beleaguered optimism, the world-weary hero ultimately returns to "cultivate his own garden." On the advice of his teacher, Pangloss, he views toiling in the garden as the most important and satisfying mission in life—occupationally, metaphorically, and esthetically.

Corsica is an island built with restraint and respect for its state as a garden, and as such has come to be viewed by the outside world as a pleasant tourist destination. People come to enjoy the spectacular physical and climatic wonders, but mainly they come for the sense of refuge Corsica offers from daily life. The human need to connect with nature's garden is at the heart of Corisca's appeal; the purity of nature's garden on Corsica also separates it from much of the "civilized" world. It is precisely this condition of "apartness and disconnectedness," this isolation of ecology from commerce, and Western civilization's 3,000-year-old notion of "conquering nature," which are the root of current environmental problems. The emergence of social and contextual changes are usually rooted in a basic revolution of philosophy. Reinforced by an eco-philosophical foundation, art can be truly effective and lead the way. For this reason, there is critical need for a fundamental shift in philosophy to one that embraces ecology as a societal as well as a nature-oriented condition of cooperative interaction.

The present ecological awareness, much a product of media promotions and consumerism, has a very short history. Frank Lloyd Wright's vision of "organic architecture," which dates to as late as the 1940s, was shaped by his astute prophetic instincts and not by the warnings of science. While major thinkers in most ancient civilizations saw nature as a chain of interrelated phenomena, as did Darwin, the motivation behind Europe's and a few American garden cities and the integration of buildings with the environment was a deep societal commitment to an earth-centric philosophy. "Learning from Corsica," as well, refers to these same traditions. The thousand years of Corsica's human history have been shaped by an instinctive sense of balance, with the ironic result that it is viewed as a recreational relic. To the contrary, it is a model for the future. The role of the arts today, especially of architectural design, is to develop an environmentally based imagery, an eco-centric technology, and a corresponding philosophy (conceivably inspired by the lessons of Corsica). If not, civilization's connection to nature will die in the mind as a symbolic force. This is the equivalent of allowing our global garden to perish from a lack of care.

A major psychological barrier to this fusion has been the notion that a new building, placed on a site, is the "big event" and seemingly dominant to everything else by virtue of its own internalized, esthetic motivations. The building is thus seen as a kind of hermetic sculptural artifact. The design is predicated on the notion that context is an annoying imposition to be tokenly acknowledged or completely ignored. Yet even so-called "contextual" architecture invariably refers to structures on which decorative and formal motifs of surrounding buildings are tacked onto the new edifice, or where a landscape architect is asked to embellish the adjacencies with a girdle of potted trees. These more superficial gestures are the polar opposite of being inspired by the models of "integrated systems" found in nature. Another problem is the way industrial societies define the use of the largest portion of land as a surface for access, usually by the automobile. In addition to destroying the natural landscape and increasing air pollution, these endless concrete arteries defeat any hope for a comfortable human scale or the development of accommodating pedestrian space. This condition is especially rampant in and around American cities, creating an artificial cityscape of environmental insensitivity.

Before these conditions can be changed for the better, both architects and urban planners and engineers are due for a good deal of serious rethinking about the way the built environment is shaped and the type of design philosophy that will be most advantageous in the future. A new sense of fusion with nature and attention to the interactive elements joining disparate parts challenge every green architect today. Some changes might evolve out of altering the way we define the built environment. In the Age of Industry and Technology, Modern buildings were about abstract design, functionalism, and sculptural form. In the Age of Information and Ecology, contemporary buildings can be seen as dialogues that serve as environmentally responsible extensions of their own contexts and as sources of narrative content and critical commentary.

One analog for rethinking the role of architectural design might be the television. Most people rarely view the TV set as a designed object, more as a container, even though it has aesthetic intentions as a piece of furniture. The container functions primarily as a filtering zone where information is processed on electronic waves and communicates these invisible pulses into readable information. In reality, the TV set is the neutral territory for filtering visual material. It is the ultimate inside-outside condition, embodied as a simultaneous package. Translating this concept into architecture, a building's sculptural volume might be reduced in importance to favor the filtering zone function of the architecture. It is the complete antithesis of Modern design principles, because it evaluates architecture based on how well a building has absorbed, then expressed and fit in with the information about its surroundings.

This idea lends credence to the notion of landscape as an intrinsic element in construction. Architects typically think of shelter as being built from such inert materials as steel, glass, and masonry, while elements of the landscape are regarded as peripheral decor. Instead, focus on architecture as the garden. It is an emphasis that includes symbolic as well as technical and aesthetic dimensions. Treating inside and outside as interactive spaces suggests that architecture, like plant life, can be seen as the product of mutable and evolutionary elements within the environment. In this way, architecture becomes a matrix, or receptacle, where vegetation is encouraged to take over structure.

To envision a building as a point of transition, from outside to inside and the reverse, extends beyond the domain of landscape to apply also to a building's walls and spaces as sources of narrative content. By avoiding the tradition of architectural design as a conversion of function into sculptural form (derivatives of Cubist or Constructivist geometry), the architect is free to explore sources of reference and communication. Design incorporates cross-referencing construction with the processes of environmental growth and change.

Earlier in this century, Frank Lloyd Wright's pioneering organic architecture used nature as a visual counterpoint to the building. The new contextualism proposes that shelter can establish a dialogue with its location to incorporate the science and spirit of plant life. It can also lead to an exchange of information that includes a structure's social and psychological context. For example, buildings can contain ritual or cosmological references; proclaim political messages; become evolutionary laboratories to promote the idea of constant change; or reflect the cybernetic revolution, where occupants can become increasingly in touch with a global rather than regional environmental network. This notion of narrative architecture suggests that the traditional preoccupation with form and space is less relevant in a world of integrated systems than the treatment of architecture as a point of transition, as an informational sponge that receives and communicates data about its surroundings. Buildings can function as monitors of philosophical change and they can be designed to provoke controversy to increase understanding about the connections between nature and the built environment.

While this message may seem far removed from the simple beauty and organic architectural traditions of an island like Corsica, the point, finally, is that this dialogue is occurring in the middle of an exemplary ECO-TEC achievement. Corsica's development over the centuries can be seen as the corrective model for an environmentally devastated industrial world. Societies can never return to the art and design achievements of history, but they can learn from history as a laboratory of methods and attitudes. Corsica's environmental balance is in part due to the island's isolation from rampant industrialization; it is indeed a relic of the past and not part of the modernized world. Yet ultimately this explanation is too simple. Within this splendid integration of shelter and landscape, in this jewel of balance with nature, lie important lessons about the reversal of industrial insanity and its doomsday scenarios. If the successful survival of the island of Corisca and the Corsican population has depended on a harmony with nature, then we can hardly risk losing the power of this wisdom under the diversionary glut of tourist brochures. If we believe that Corsica is a passive resort, merely a place of leisurely escape, a sentimental fragment of the past, then we are confessing that an industrialized apocalypse is our only choice for the future. This is a grim prospect our children may not survive.

James Wines, architect, is principal of SITE architects in New York City and one of the earliest proponents for a "green" architecture.

Nonza, Cap Corse, Corsica (Storefront for Art and Architecture).

Revegetation of Asbestos Mine Wastes

Alan. J. M. Baker

The first visit to the derelict asbestos mine workings and processing plant at Canari, Cap Corse, occurred on June 26–27,
1993, by Dr. A. J. M. Baker (University of Sheffield, UK), Dr. T.
Meredith (McGill University, Canada), and Mr. B. Thomas (New
York Environmental Health Department). Their purpose was to
assess the current state of the natural revegetation of the site and
to suggest prescriptive measures for further waste stabilization
and site remediation through revegetation.

Site description

The Canari site has been derelict since 1965 although there has
been subsequent small-scale geochemical exploration for potentially economic deposits of nickel. The plant complex comprises
a massive opencast working high above the factory, mine
wastes, tailings, and processing wastes, and more consolidated
materials in the vicinity of the factory. The majority of waste
materials from the processing plant were tipped directly into the
sea, or used for building the artificial beach at Albo. The opencast was worked by terraces and was galleried; it is now used ille-
gally for domestic waste tipping. Piles of coarse ultramafic waste
rock surround the area. Above and around the factory the steep
hillside is built up of fine asbestos wastes and tailings produced

Asbestos plant, Canari (Tam Miller).

by the processing works. This white, loose, powdery material has formed surface crusts which are superficially more stable than the underlying deposits. There is evidence, however, of massive erosion and gullying from washout during rain storms. These wastes are clearly unstable and prone to dispersion by wind and water erosion. A level area in front of the factory comprises compacted wastes and, at the time of this writing, is the site of a restaurant, a timber mill, and a small ceramics works. It is bounded by the sea cliffs which are now essentially composed of mineral wastes and are equally unstable.

Extent of natural revegetation

The site has been abandoned for over 30 years and a portion of the wastes around the workings are much older. It is not surprising, therefore, that some degree of plant colonization, particularly in the more stable areas, has occurred. The different areas around the site include:

1. *Coarse wastes around the opencast:* The rocky terrain is generally inimical to plant colonization, and the majority of the wastes are devoid of vegetation cover except where material was crushed to produce finer particles, such as on the perimeter trackways and paths. A notable plant which is capable of growing in virtually all situations here is *Helichrysum italicum* (Immortelle), which forms a large shrubby cushion and roots deeply into the substratum. There is evidence of large numbers of annual grasses and small herbs (mostly legumes) along and beside the tracks. One perennial, tussock-forming grass, Dactylis glomerata, is prominent. Occasional perennial herbs and sub-shrubs include *Daucus carrota, Glaucium flavum, Dittrichia viscosa, Psoralea bituminosa,* and *Thymus.*

2. *Fine wastes and tailings beside and above the factory:* An overall sparse cover of vegetation is apparent especially on the steeply-sloping fine wastes close to the works. Where there is some stability, as for example on more level terraces and ledges, there is more extensive colonization by maquis species. This is also the case at less recently disturbed areas at the margins of the site. A few woody species such as fig (*Ficus carica*) and the spiny leguminous shrubs *Calycotome* and *Genista* corsica appear to root directly into the loose asbestos wastes; others can colo-

nize the gullied and eroded channels, such as Dittrichia viscosa and the coastal species *Crithmum maritimum* and *Limonium patrimoniense*. *Cynodon dactylon* (Bermuda grass) a creeping, mat-forming grass, was noted on the loose wastes, together with a more tufted grass, *Hyparrhenia hirta*. The older, more stable slopes are characterized by coarser material mixed with fine wastes, supporting a greater range of species with increased overall cover; these include small trees and shrubs of Kermes oak (*Quercus coccifera*), lentisk (*Pistacia lentiscus*), juniper (*Juniperus phoenicea*), and those already noted.

3. *Consolidated waste on level ground in front of the factory:* This area supports the greatest diversity of plants and a more extensive cover of vegetation than in the other areas. A mixture of annual and perennial species of the maritime, maquis, and ruderal elements are found here. *Helichrysum italicum* is prominent and the commonest maquis plant; others include *Dittrichia viscosa*, various rockroses (*Cistus*), *Thymelaea hirusta*, rosemary (*Rosmarinus officinalis*), *Asphodelus,* and *Euphorbia characias*. Coastal plants include: *Daucus carrota, Crithmum maritimum, Glaucium flavum, Juncus acutus, Plantago coronopus, Spergularia,* and *Frankenia laevis*. The remaining cover is made up of dead annual grasses and legumes (e.g. *Lotus*), and perennial herbs such as the legume *Psoralea bituminosa*, the thistle *Scolymus hispanicus,* and the grass *Cynodon dactylon*.

4. *Possible revegetation strategies:* Any long-term revegetation program must aim to facilitate the reinstatement of an adapted, perennial plant cover in order to stabilize the wastes and prevent further erosion. The underlying problems in establishing a vigorous plant cover on ultramafic asbestos wastes at Canari could include:

—Extreme nutrient deficiencies, particularly of nitrogen (N) and phosphorus (P);

—Adverse calcium (Ca) /magnesium (Mg) balance;

—Low organic matter status;

—Possible toxicities due to high concentrations of nickel (Ni), chromium (Cr) and sometimes cobalt (Co);

—Drought problems arising from both the physical nature and texture of the substratum as well as the climatic regime.

The brief survey undertaken suggests that the overwhelming

problem for plant colonization is drought, exacerbated locally by slope instability, and low organic and nutrient status. From the range of widespread plant colonists observed on the asbestos wastes it seems unlikely that metal toxicities are serious. However, a full survey of the variation in substratum conditions over the entire site, both physical and chemical, is a prerequisite for any revegetation program.

The initial site survey has revealed a number of possible plant colonists of these extreme physico-chemical conditions. The majority are maquis plants which are well-adapted, stress-tolerators. It is a realistic goal, therefore, to restore maquis vegetation over the site. The survey also revealed at least three perennial grasses which can establish directly on or in the wastes and which offer considerable potential for surface stabilization, especially *Cynodon dactylon* because of its creeping stems and mat-forming habit. Some perennial legume species were also notable as early colonizers (e.g. *Psoralea bituminosa*). Such species are able to fix atmospheric nitrogen and thus increase the N-status of the system, a strongly limiting factor in further plant colonization.

A two phase approach could thus be contemplated:

1. Establishing potentially fast-growing grasses, such as *Cynodon*, together with legumes and other stress-tolerant herbs on to the bare asbestos wastes and unstable slopes. Hydroseeding would probably be the most successful technique, in which commercial seed of the target species is introduced on to the remote slopes in a slurry of an organic matrix such as sewage sludge and cellulose binder supplemented with additional nutrients, by pumping under pressure. There are well-established protocols for this type of reseeding approach (see sources). The sewage sludge and organic matrix 'sticks,' or adheres the seed innoculum on to unstable surfaces and allows the seed to become embedded on to areas which are not easily seeded manually. The timing of such an operation is critical in view of the potential drought conditions likely to prevail at Canari. Autumn could be the most suitable time for seeding in order to optimize chances for successful germination and seedling establishment when water supplies are adequate.

2. The direct introduction and establishment of young, nurs-

ery-grown plants of maquis species, which are known to survive on the wastes. Planting would require an organic matrix such as a peat medium in the root zone to assist in water retention and nutrient provision; irrigation may also be needed in the early transplant stages. Autumn planting might again be preferable to spring.

To enhance the possibility for successful transplantation, plants derived from local provenances should be used.

Conclusions

The suggested revegetation strategies could provide a technique for gradual stabilization and greening of the asbestos wastes at Canari. Major capital investment would be required particularly for the hydroseeding work and nursery cultivation of maquis plants for transplantation. Irrigation might also be costly, and subsequent maintenance and replanting may be necessary, all of which are hidden costs. Above all, the economic cost of revegetation must be considered in the context of human, environmental, and safety costs of leaving the asbestos wastes to revegetate naturally at a very slow rate.

Preliminary trial work should proceed to ascertain the characteristics of the site and the substratum, the optimum conditions for species establishment, and subsequent maintenance. These could take the form of glasshouse pot trials using Canari wastes, and might be developed to a further pilot field stage before large-scale revegetation work would be implemented.

Postscript on the Canari Project

The efforts of ECO-TEC together with pressure exerted by concerned communities around the Canari site were pivotal in convincing the French government to address a long neglected environmental problem. After the initial analysis of the site by the ECO-TEC team, the government requested a report detailing the geology and history of the Canari mining site and the environmental impact and risk of the industrial slags. This impressive study, by Yves Paquette of INERIS (Institute National de l'Environment et des Risques), was presented at the 1995 ECO-TEC forum. At the 1996 forum, other independent remediation proposals were considered. Paul Casalonga, a Unesco consultant, called for an ecological museum of mining. Another proposal by a group of Italian Ecological engineers from the Biology Department of Turin University, headed by Marco Orsi of Consulagri S.r.l., suggested a low-cost experimental method to cover the exposed disturbed ground, where the native maquis plants were scanty and slow to reproduce, with fast-growing vines and grasses. Even more significant was the independent formation of a locally based watchdog organization, the Canari Committee, representing the community's different political perspectives, which is now overseeing the remediation of this site.

T. R. Moore and R. C. Zimmermann, "Establishment of vegetation on serpentine asbestos mine wastes, Southeastern Quebec, Canada," *Journal of Applied Ecology* 14 (1977): 589–599.

T. R. Moore and R. C. Zimmermann, "Follow-up studies of vegetation establishment on asbestos tailings in Southeastern Quebec," *Reclamation Review* 2 (1979): 143–146.

D. R. Meyer, "Nutritional problems associated with the establishment of vegetation on tailings from an asbestos mine," *Environmental Pollution Series A* 23 (1980): 287–298.

J. C. Leroy, "How to establish and maintain growth on tailings in Canada—cold winters and short growing seasons," in *Tailings Disposal Today*, edited by Aplin & Argall (San Francisco: Miller Freeman, 1973), 411–447.

J. A. Quilty, "Guidelines for rehabilitation for tailings dumps and open cuts," *Journal of Soil Conservation* 31 (1975): 95–107.

R. F. Smith and B. L. Kay, "Revegetation of serpentine soils: difficult but not impossible," *California Agriculture* 40 (Jan/Feb, 1986): 18–19.

Alan J.M. Baker is Senior Lecturer and Environmental Consultant at the University of Sheffield, UK.

West Coast, Cap Corse view surrounding the Canari asbestos factory (StoreFront for Art and Architecture).

ALAN J. M. BAKER

Heartfelt:
A Site-Specific Portrait
Mel Chin

I. Site and Team Selection

A. Select a site where there is a sheep raising tradition.

B. Establish a collaboration between the population of that locality, an ecologist from the area, and a fabric specialist familiar with natural dyes and wool.

    1. Document and catalogue indigenous historical motifs (architectural and artistic, family crests, folk tales, etc.) to provide a bank of visual and folkloric images.

    2. Consult with a scholar of linguistics and anthropology to understand the cultural origins or "roots" of the site.

The collaborative team goes out into the field to catalogue and make "cross pollinating" notes regarding the flora and fauna. The team should assess the ecological health of the site, determine native sources for natural dyes and compare scientific knowledge and folk understanding.

II. Evaluation

Based on data collected by the collaborative team, local conditions, resources, and desires will be assessed to determine whether to proceed with the second stage of HEARTFELT.

Corsican plant, Lotus corniculatus (Tam Miller).

Corsican traffic symbol and its replica in felt. The felt was produced and dyed by hand, using local wool and plants, during the Heartfelt project (Mel Chin).

HEARTFELT

III. Collect and Prepare Raw Materials from the Site
A. Wool

B. Plants for the dye stock

Note: Although HEARTFELT is designed with the island of Corsica in mind, its application could be in any locality where appropriate conditions and desires prevail.

IV. Produce an Artifact:
Blanket, Coat or Hats, as a Site Specific Portrait

A. Create another collaborative team of interested people from the community and experts in traditional felt making and organize a felt making and dying workshop.

Suggestions: Look to other cultures with felt-making traditions (such as Mid-Eastern wool cloak makers or Mongolian felt rug/yurt makers) that may be related to contemporary Corsicans (this linkage established through the preliminary linguistic and anthropologic investigations). Bring selected felt-makers to the area to lead a workshop. Interested community members could decide on patterns and colors or designs could be pulled from the bank of images.

V. Other Initiatives and Projections [after stages]

A. Possible economic outcomes:

    1. A self-sustaining, low-tech method of producing articles of use to the community is Investigated.

    2. Future marketing of these articles (to fashion industry or to collectors as art objects) could establish another economic incentive.

B. Possible ecologic/educational outcome:

    1. A greater understanding of and respect for the ecologic potential of a site.

    2. Expanded awareness through a sharing of ideas and methods.

    3. Collection of data and sharing of information may spur ideas for related projects.

FRENCH	les Carottes (flowers)	Color : light yellow
LATIN	Daucus	*Notes : used traditionally as dye*
ENGLISH	Wild Carrot	

FRENCH	Ciste de Montpellier (buds)	Color : bright golden yellow
LATIN	Cistus	*Notes : buds & leaves of other*
CORSICAN	mucchiu	*Ciste variety gave brighter yellow*

LATIN	Bellardia trixago (seed cases)	Color : drab olive green

FRENCH	Garance (roots)	Color : red/orange-red
LATIN	Rubia	*Notes : well-known traditional dye used in*
CORSICAN	apiccamanu	*England, France and America*
ENGLISH	Madder	

FRENCH	Bruyere (root)	Color : pink-brown/brown
LATIN	Erica arborea	
CORSICAN	scope	
ENGLISH	Heather	

LATIN	Rhamnus alaternus	Color : bluish green/light bright green
ENGLISH	Persian berries	*Notes : powdered berries used*
		traditionally as dye

FRENCH	myrte (berries)	Color : blue/black
LATIN	Mrytus	*Notes : traditionally used in Corsica as dye*
CORSICAN	morta	*and for jam and liquor; berries ripen in*
ENGLISH	myrtle	*late fall to winter*

FRENCH	Arbousier (fruit)	Color : red
LATIN	Arbutus	*Notes : Used in Corsica for jam*
CORSICAN	arbitru, arbidu	
ENGLISH	strawberry tree	

Corsican plant, Cistus monspeliensis *(Tam Miller).*

Les derniers mots: Lessons and Applications from Corsica

Kyong Park

In 1991, Amerigo Marras, Jean Pierre Vernet, and Roy Pelletier came to me with a proposal for ECO-TEC. Since then, we have collaborated on several projects and conferences, in Corsica and New York City. These combine a multi-disciplinary and international process to develop a close relationship between two primal and powerful forces of the environment: ecology that determines the length of human existence, and technology that outlines how we will live during that period.

From the first event in Corsica, our ideal and abstract pursuits intermingled with the estranged yet powerful history of the island, which has been governed by France since the French bought it from Genoa three centuries ago.

First there is the democratic tradition of Corsican politics, which was long ago established by Pascal Paoli, the father of the Corsican Nation. Paoli realized, for a brief moment, independence for Corsica and led his democratic government to create a human rights bill that predated the American and French Revolutions. Napoleon Bonaparte was another significant Corsican who, despite his diplomatic talents and achievements outside the island, did nothing for Corsica itself. These historical figures embody the strength of the Corsican mind and character. They also reflect the dichotomy of Corsica's relation to the

Convent de l'Annonication, in which ECO-TEC conferences in Corsica were held (Jean Pierre Vernet).

continent and the rest of the world, which continues to be manifest in the violence of nationalist movements.

The indigenous strength of Corsica made its presence felt on ECO-TEC proceedings. The specific nature of Corsica began to override the participants' distant origins. In fact, we designed forum events to respond to Corsican contexts and needs, as reflex, thus reversing the exploitation of a marginal culture by dominant interventions. At my first presentation in Corsica, I spoke of creating an onsite center for research and development of ecology and technology. Since then, the role of StoreFront has been to convene international participants through forums and conferences, and find ways to apply their expertise to indigenous sources and needs. Collaborative projects have developed over time in which local and international experts work together with students to develop methods to respond to environmental crises, and to apply solutions. The center has come to function as a bridge between theory and practice, and the collaborative work also benefits Corsica's landscape and culture.

This anthology summarizes some of the work that forms the foundation of this center. It also reflects future possibilities of StoreFront, as we look toward developing concrete applications of the ideas that have been and will be presented.

Kyong Park is the Founder of StoreFront for Art and Architecture and was its Director from 1982–1998.

Avant-Travaux Paris-based architectural collaborative, brainchildren of Paul Virilio.

Alan J.M. Baker Senior Lecturer and Environmental Consultant at the University of Sheffield, UK.

Baubiologie (see Wolf Dieter Blank)

Wolf Dieter Blank Ecological design engineer associated with the Baubiologie Institute, Germany.

Paul Casalonga Architect, expert on traditional habitats, UNESCO consultant, based in Corsica.

Pierre Chaubon Commissioner of the Environment for a European Community and Mayor of a Corsican village.

Mel Chin Sculptor, whose work focuses on political and ecological tragedies.

Manuel de Landa Filmmaker and author of *War in the Age of Intelligent Machines* and *A Thousand Years of Non Linear History*.

Neil Denari Architect; director of Southern California Institute of Architecture.

Mark Dery Cultural critic; author of *Escape Velocity: Cyberculture at the End of the Century*, and *The Pyrotechnic Insanitarium: Madness and Mayhem in Millennial America*.

Dennis Dollens Architectural writer and publisher of *Sites* magazine and *Lumen*

Claude Faure Artist, associated with Cité des Sciences et de l'Industrie de la Villette, Paris.

Foresight Institute (see Kathleen Shatter)

Jean Gardner Author of *Urban Wilderness: Nature in New York City*, and professor of History and Theory, Department of Architecture and Environmental Design, Parsons School of Design.

Felix Guattari Philosopher, died in 1992; author of Chaosmose, and co-author with Gilles Deleuze of major studies on contemporary culture, notably *A Thousand Plateaus*.

Richard Kahan Urban developer; chairman of the Riverside South Planning Corporation, which oversees community and public interest matters related to the development of Trump City.

Cindi Katz Teaches at the Center for the Critical Analysis of Contemporary Culture, in Geography at Rutgers University, and Environmental Psychology and Cultural Studies at the City University of New York; coeditor with Janice Monk of *Full Circles: Geographies of Women over the Life Course.*

Eric Kiviat Professor of Ecology at Bard College; founder and executive director of Hudsonia, an institute dedicated to the preservation of the Hudson River.

Shaun Lovejoy Professor of Physics, McGill University in Montreal, Canada.

Richard Lowenberg Architect and telemedia consultant; director of Infozone at Telluride Institute, Colorado.

Neil Lutzen Landscape architect; proponent of alternative development and management of water systems.

Paul Mankiewicz Director of Gaia Institute in New York.

Gianfranco Mantegna Art curator and writer based in New York

Amerigo Marras Architect and curator. He is the founder of ECO-TEC. He has produced multimedia cultural events since 1973.

Thomas Meredith Professor in the Department of Geography, McGill University, Montreal.

Tam Miller Artist and writer based in New York.

Yves Nacher Architect, Director of the French Institute of Architects, and the World Association of Architects.

Helen Nagge Editor.

Lois Nesbitt New York-based artist and writer.

Shirin Neshat Visual artist.

Marco Orsi Architect and director of the ecological rehabilitation firm Consulagri, in Turin, Italy.

Ove Arup New York-based engineering firm specializing in ecologically sustainable buildings.

Yves Paquette Geologist, associated with the INERIS, a Paris-based research center on geology.

Kyong Park Architect. Founder and director of StoreFront for Art & Architecture, New York.

Roy Pelletier Architect, based in Toronto, Canada.

Richard Plunz Professor of Architecture and Director of Urban Design Program, Columbia University; author of numerous studies on physical and social design.

Mahadev Raman Engineer, associate of Ove Arup & Partners.

Andrew Ross Director of American Studies program at New York University; author of *Strange Weather: Culture, Science and Technology in the Age of Limits, No Respect, The Chicago Gangster Theory of Life*, and other publications. He is coeditor of the journal *Social Text*.

Kathleen Shatter Information manager for Foresight Institute, which specializes in the education of nanotechnology, founded by Arthur Drexler.

Leslie Sherr Writer based in New York.

Babu Thomas Environmental engineer, New York Department of Environmental Protection, City Of New York

José Tomasi Teacher and director of Department of Plastic Arts and Applied Arts at the Université de Corse, Corsica.

Jean Pierre Vernet Geologist, director of Association for the Conservation of the Architectural Patrimony and director of ECO-TEC Corse, Corsica.

Constantin von Barlowen Scholar of anthropology and ethnography; director of the Institute for Comparative Cultures in Munich, Germany.

Mark Wigley Author of architectural theory and history; *Derrida's Haunt: Architecture of Deconstruction*.

Tod Williams & Billie Tsien Architects, principals of architectural and design partnership since 1986.

James Wines Architect; principal of SITE architects in New York City.